The New Lexicon-Webster DICTIONARY for Children

Editorial Director
  DONALD D. WOLF

Consultant
  DONALD O. BOLANDER,
  M.A., Litt.D.

Design and Layout
  MARGOT L. WOLF

Published by
LEXICON PUBLICATIONS, INC.
387 Park Avenue South, New York, NY 10016

Note to Parents

This book is your child's first step into the world of dictionaries.

The Lexicon editors have done their best to make this first step an exciting one, helpful to the child in advancing easily and comfortably to the next level of dictionaries.

This new Lexicon-Webster Dictionary for Children is the result of the wide knowledge and experience of our editorial staff. We are well versed in lexicography since we have been in the word business for many years, producing major encyclopedias and dictionaries for everyone in the family.

The more than 1,300 words and definitions in this edition were taken from our adult New Lexicon-Webster Dictionary of the English Language and were selected and prepared editorially for an age level of five through nine years.

More than 900 full-color illustrations are included to attract and entertain your child, to help in understanding the meaning of the words, and to bring him or her to the book time and time again. Together, the definitions and color illustrations will enable your child to learn with little effort.

It will be helpful for your child and at the same time may be fun for you to sit together and read the dictionary aloud.

We are sure that once your child spends time with this book, he or she will understand that dictionaries are not forbidding, but useful and often delightful books to read, while at the same time building the vocabulary.

The Publishers

A a

above

At night I can see the stars **above** me.
The stars in the sky are **over** my head.

absent

Tom was **absent** from school today.
Tom **did not come** to school today.

accident

Tom and Bob have had an **accident.**
They ran into each other on their bicycles.

accordion

Jim plays the **accordion** very well.
He makes music by squeezing it.

across

Joe lives **across** the street from me.
His house is **on the other side** of the street.

add

Add my apple to your apple and we have two apples.
When we **add,** we put things together.

afraid

Don't be **afraid** of the lion.
He cannot get out of his cage.

after

Mary is behind me in the line.
She is **after** me.

afternoon

School is dismissed in the **afternoon.**
The time from noon until dark is **afternoon.**

again

Mother and I went to the store **again.**
We went shopping **once more.**

air

Air is all around us.
Ann blows **air** into the balloon.

airplane

Your daddy goes on a trip in an **airplane.**
He flies to another city.

airport

Yesterday we went to the **airport.**
We saw airplanes coming in and going out.

album

Peter has taken some pictures with his camera.
He sticks them in an **album,** a book with blank pages.

alike

Mary and I wear the same dress.
We dress just **alike.**

alive

We have two plants on the windowsill in our classroom.
One plant is **alive.** The other plant is dead.

all
The teacher took **all** the children to the zoo.
Every child in her class went along.

allow
Tom hit the ball over the fence.
Will the man **allow** us to get it?

alphabet
Do you know the letters of the **alphabet?**
Look for them in the picture.

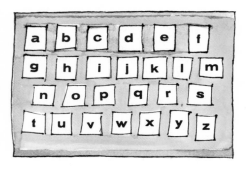

also
My friend is **also** going to the movies.
She is going to the movies **too.**

always
My sister **always** helps me with my homework.
She helps me **every time.**

among
My house is **among** some trees.
It is in the middle of the trees.

amuse

Our book has some very funny stories.
They **amuse** us very much.

anchor

What a big **anchor** this is! It will make the boat stay still in the water.

angry

Jill was **angry** when someone took her book.
She did not like losing it; it made her **mad.**

animal

An **animal** is any living thing that is not a plant.
A dog is a four-legged **animal;** a man is a two-legged **animal.**

answer

When the teacher calls on you, you **answer.**
You tell her what she wants to know.

ant

An **ant** is a busy little insect.
One **ant** helps another **ant** to find food.

antenna

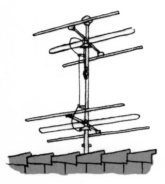

The **antenna** on our roof brings the picture to our television set.

any

Dick did not eat **any** supper.
He ate **no** supper at all.
Jane can wear **any** dress. She can wear **the one she chooses.**

appear

The stars **appear** in the sky at night.
They **can be seen** when it is dark.

apple

The **apple** is a round, red fruit.
I like to eat **apples.**

apricot

The **apricot** grows in warm places. It is yellow and juicy, something like a small peach.

April

April is the fourth month of the year. It is a spring month and sometimes very rainy.

apron

Mother wears an **apron** when she cooks and cleans.
It helps to keep her dress clean.

aquarium

We keep five goldfish in our **aquarium.**

architect

An **architect** designs homes and big office buildings.
He plans them and makes drawings for the builders to follow.

argue

The girls **argue** over what to play. They do not want to play the same game.

arithmetic

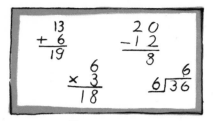

At school we study **arithmetic.**
We learn to add, to subtract, to multiply, and to divide.

arm

My **arm** is the part of my body from the hand to the shoulder.
My **arm** rests on the **arm** of the chair.

ashamed

Mary was **ashamed** of herself.
She felt sorry for acting rudely.

ask

When I **ask** my teacher a question, she helps me to find the answer.

asleep

The children are all **asleep** at nap time.
They are **not awake.**

aster

The **aster** is a flower shaped like a star.
It grows in many colors.

atlas

An **atlas** is a book of maps.
We can find all the countries of the world in the **atlas.**

August

August is the eighth month of the year. It is usually very hot in **August.**

autumn

Autumn is the season between summer and winter.
It is also called **fall.**

aunt

My **aunt** Alice came to see us.
My **aunt** is my mother's or my father's sister.

awake

The children are all **awake** after nap time.
They are **not asleep.**

ax

An **ax** is a cutting tool.
It is used to chop down trees or to split logs for the fireplace.

B b

baboon

A **baboon** is a large monkey. It has a short tail and a nose and mouth like a dog's.

baby

A **baby** is a very young person. We have to feed and wash the **baby** and take good care of him.

back

We ride on the **back** of the pony. The **back** of the book is the part near the end.

bad

Jim did not do what the teacher said. He was a **bad** boy.

bag

When I go to the store, the grocer puts the things I buy in a **bag.**

baggage

We packed our clothes to go on a trip.
Our **baggage** is ready to be put in the car.

bake

I like to watch Mother **bake** cakes and cookies and pies. Sometimes I help her.

baker

The **baker** wears a white coat and a tall white hat when he is working.

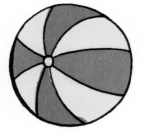

ball

This is my big beach **ball.**
My brother plays lots of games with **balls.**

balloon

Mary did not hold onto her **balloon.**
The wind is blowing it high in the sky.

banana

A **banana** is a long yellow fruit.
Bananas grow in big bunches on trees.

band

Tom plays the drum in the school **band.**
Other children play other instruments.

bandage

A **bandage** is a clean cloth to cover cuts or scrapes.
I can put on a tape **bandage** myself.

bang

A **bang** is a loud noise.
A firecracker makes a big **bang.**

bank

The **bank** of the river is sandy here.
It is like being at the beach.

bank

My piggy **bank** has a slot in the top so that I can save my nickels and dimes in it.

bar

A **bar** of candy is a nice treat.
The lion's cage at the zoo has strong **bars.**

bark

The **bark** is the outside part of a tree.
When my dog sees a cat he **barks.**

barn

A **barn** is a building on a farm.
The farmer keeps his cows and horses in the **barn** and stores hay in the hayloft.

barometer

The **barometer** measures the air pressure.
It tells us what kind of weather is coming.

barrel

A **barrel** is round and made of wood or metal.
It can hold cider or nails.

baseball

Baseball is a game played by two teams.
They take turns trying to hit the ball with a bat.

basement

A **basement** is the lowest part of a building.
We have a **basement** at the bottom of our house.

basket

A **basket** is used for carrying things.
It may be small for little packages, or big for laundry.

basketball

Basketball is a game played by two teams. They take turns trying to throw the ball into a hoop.

bat

A **bat** is a small animal that flies at night. It looks like a mouse with wings of skin.

bathe

It is hot and sunny today. We are going to **bathe** in the pond to keep cool.

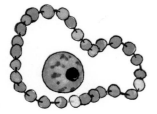

beach

A **beach** is the sandy slope of the ocean or a lake.
It is a great place to swim and make sand castles.

bead

A **bead** is a tiny ball with a hole through it for stringing.

beans

Beans are a vegetable.
Some kinds of beans are **string beans, lima beans,** and **kidney beans.**

bear

The **bear** is a large, furry animal.
This **bear** is licking honey that he has found in a bees' nest in the tree.

beautiful

This is a **beautiful** scene in the mountains.
I like to look at **pretty** scenes.

beaver

The **beaver** is a small, furry animal with a big flat tail.
It chews down small trees to make a dam in a stream.

bed

We sleep best if we lie down on a **bed.**
The gardener digs the soil to make a flower **bed.**

bee

A **bee** is an insect that makes wax and honey.
It has four wings and a stinger. It gets its food from flowers.

beet

A **beet** is a vegetable.
Red **beets** are good to eat. White **beets** can be made into sugar when they are crushed.

beetle

A **beetle** is an insect with a hard back that covers fine wings.
This **beetle** is a June bug.
Other **beetles** are black, blue, or green.

before

A comes **before** B in the alphabet.
A is **ahead of** B.

beg

My dog likes to **beg** at the table.
He asks me to give him bits of food.

behave

I try to **behave** well.
I try to do just what Mother wants me to do.

behind

A good dog walks just **behind** its owner.
It walks **in back** of him.

bell

Our church has an old **bell.**
When the **bell** rings we know it is almost time for church.

belong

My toys **belong** to me.
They are mine.
I **own** them.

below

The roots of a tree are **below** the ground.
They grow **under** the ground.

belt

Jeffrey's **belt** is made of brown leather.
He wears it to hold his pants up.

bench

There is a green **bench** in our yard.
We sit on it to play games on
sunny days.

bend

Can you **bend** down and touch your
toes? A **bend** is a curve or a turn.

berry

A **berry** is a small juicy fruit.
It is fun to pick **strawberries** and
blackberries and **blueberries** in the
summer.

best

I am wearing my **best** dress. It is the
nicest one I have.

better

Jim does **better** than Joe in school.
Jim gets higher grades.

between

Lunch comes **between**
breakfast and dinner.
It is in the **middle.**

bicycle

This is my first **bicycle.**
I am allowed to ride it on the
sidewalk.

big

The elephant is a **big** animal.
It is very **large.**

binoculars

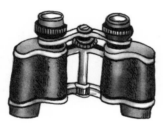

Binoculars are a small
telescope for two eyes.
We look through
binoculars to see
faraway things clearly.

birch

It is easy to tell a **birch** tree. It has a
white trunk.

bird

This bluejay is a kind of **bird.**
A **bird** is an animal with wings and
feathers.

birthday

Today is John's **birthday.**
He is ten years old.
Mother made this **birthday**
cake for him.

bite

These two dogs are fighting.
They **bite** each other with sharp teeth.

blackberry

A **blackberry** is a
small juicy fruit that
grows on a thorny
bush.
We like to eat
blackberry jelly and
blackberry pie.

blackboard

The teacher puts our
homework on the
blackboard.
She writes on the
black slate with
white chalk.

blanket

My baby brother has a soft
wool **blanket.**
It keeps him snug and warm.

blind

This man is **blind.**
He cannot see.
He carries a white cane.
The Seeing Eye dog helps him.

block

My best friend lives in the next
block.
His house is in the next **street.**
My little brother builds things out of
blocks.

blood

Bob has cut himself.
Blood is coming from the cut.

blouse

Helen is wearing a pretty red
blouse.
A girl's **blouse** is something like a
boy's shirt.

blow

A strong wind can **blow** a tree down.
I can put out a candle by **blowing** on
it.

blue

Blue is the color of the sky.
Some people have **blue** eyes.

blueberry

A **blueberry** is a small juicy fruit.
My mother makes **blueberry muffins** and **blueberry** pie.

board

A **board** is a long, flat piece of wood.
We can use this **board** to make a seesaw.

boast

Harry likes to **boast** that he has a fine bicycle.
He likes to **brag** about how great he is.

boat

A **boat** is a craft used for traveling on water.
It may be small, like a canoe, or large, like an ocean liner.

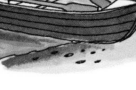

boil

Mother puts the kettle on the stove to **boil.**
When the water is bubbling, she uses it to make tea.

bone

My dog likes to chew on a **bone.**
The **bones** in our bodies help us to stand and walk.

book

This is my **book** of fairy tales.
It is full of fine stories with colored pictures.

bookcase

I have my very own **bookcase.**
I keep all my school books and story books in it.

boots

We all wear **boots** on rainy or snowy days to keep our feet dry and warm.

bottle

A **bottle** is usually made of glass.
It holds liquids.

bottom

The **bottom** of a thing is the lowest part.
The earth under a pond is the **bottom** of the pond. The last line on this page is the **bottom** of the page.

bounce

Susan throws the ball against the wall.
Watch it **bounce** back to her.

bow

You can make a **bow** out of a strong stick.
The string has to be pulled tight and fastened firmly.

bowl

A **bowl** is a deep, round dish.
A big outdoor sport field is also called a **bowl** because of its shape.

box

I made this **box** myself. It is made of cardboard and covered with colored paper.
I keep my stamps in it.

Boy Scout

My brother John is a **Boy Scout.** He wears this uniform when he meets with his Scout troop.

bracelet

A bracelet is worn around the wrist.
Girls wear pretty **bracelets.**
Boys sometimes wear **bracelets** with their name or initials.

brake

When we come to a stoplight, my father steps on the **brake** to stop the car.

brave

Jack is very **brave.**
He is **not afraid** to try to do hard things.

bread

This is a loaf of rye **bread.**
I also like wholewheat **bread** and white **bread.**

break

A window is easy to **break.**
Dishes and glasses also **break** very easily.

breakfast

We are having **breakfast** in the garden.
The **first meal** of the day tastes good in the sunshine.

breathe

All human beings and animals must **breathe**.
They cannot live without **drawing in air.**

breeze

The leaves flutter in the **breeze**.
It is a **gentle wind** that makes them move.

brick

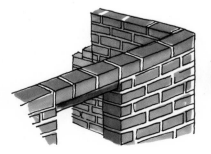

A **brick** is a building block made from clay.
Walls and houses and chimneys are built with **bricks.**

bridge

The long **bridge** carries cars and trucks and people across the water.
Some **bridges** also carry trains.

bright

It is a **bright** day today.
The sun is shining in a clear blue sky.

bring

Daddy promised to **bring** me a present tonight.
He will carry home something that I will like.

broccoli

Broccoli is a green vegetable.
It looks like tiny flowers on a stalk.

brook

A **brook** is a narrow little stream.
Some **brooks** get larger as they flow and become rivers.

brother

In our family there are four children. My **brother** Peter is the youngest.

brown

Brown is a dark color.
The earth and the trunks of trees are **brown.**

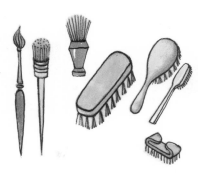

brush

A **brush** does many jobs. Can you find the **paintbrush,** the **hairbrush,** and the **toothbrush?**

buds

The chestnut **buds** are getting big. They will soon burst open and grow into leaves and flowers.

buffalo

This is an American **buffalo.**
It is a large, sturdy animal.

build

John and Mary **build** castles and bridges with their blocks.
Workmen **build** houses for people to live in.

bull

My uncle has a large **bull** on his cattle ranch.
Some **bulls** are fierce.

bumblebee

A **bumblebee** is a large, hairy kind of bee.
When a **bumblebee** flies, it makes a loud and deep humming noise.

bump

You have given yourself a bad **bump** running into the tree.
An uneven place in the road is called a **bump.**

bunch

Some fruits grow in a **bunch,** like bananas or grapes.
I picked a lot of flowers and put them together in a **bunch.**

burn

The sun is so hot that it will **burn** my skin.
A fire may **burn** a house down.

burst

What a bang! My bicycle tire has **burst.**

A water pipe **burst** in our street and made a flood.

bury

My dog likes to **bury** a bone in the yard and then dig it up.

My aunt **buries** bulbs in the garden to grow into spring flowers.

bus

This is a sightseeing **bus.** It has big windows and a plastic roof to see through.

bush

A **bush** is a low leafy plant, smaller than a tree.

Roses and azaleas grow on **bushes.**

busy

The workman is **busy** digging up the street.

He is working hard to repair the street.

butcher

Josephine is buying meat from the **butcher.** He cuts the meat into the size pieces her mother wants.

butter

Butter is a food made from milk. **Butter** is very good to spread on bread and also on corn and potatoes.

butterfly

A **butterfly** is a beautiful insect.
Butterflies come in many brilliant colors.

button

A **button** is used to fasten clothes together.
Buttons may be big and fancy or small and not meant to be seen.

buy

Jim went to the store to **buy** a lollipop. He gave the storekeeper some money and got the candy in exchange.

 **C c**

cabbage

Cabbage is a vegetable that we eat cooked or raw.
We boil **cabbage**, or we slice it fine and make coleslaw.

cabin

My uncle has a **cabin** in the mountains. Last summer we lived in it on our vacation.

cactus

The **cactus** grows in the desert. A **cactus plant** can be as small as a thimble or as large as a tree.

cage

Wild animals like the lion are kept in **cages** at the zoo.

cake

Mother baked a **cake** for my birthday. She used flour and eggs and sugar and chocolate.

calendar

The **calendar** tells us what day of the week it is, and what month of the year.

calf

A **calf** is a baby cow.
Baby elephants and whales are also called **calves.**

call

Mother asked me to **call** my sister to come in the house.
Sometimes I **call** my father on the telephone.

camel

The **camel** is a large animal with a humped back.
Some kinds of **camels** have two humps.

camera

Bill wants to take some pictures of us. He is learning how to use his new **camera.**

camp

When we go to summer **camp** we sleep in a tent.
We play outdoors and hike and swim.

can

Mary **can** run fast.
She **is able** to run fast.
Some foods come in a **can** to keep them fresh.

Canada

Canada is the country to the north of the United States.
Canadians speak English or French.

Canada goose

The **Canada goose** is one of the biggest birds in North America.
Canada geese also live in the United States.

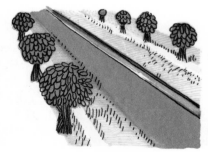

canal

A **canal** is a waterway made by men.
It goes straight across the country.

candle

I like to see a **candle** burning. It makes the room look cheerful and warm.

candy

Candy is a sweet treat. It is made with sugar and other flavors like chocolate or mint.

cannot

Harry **cannot** climb the tree. He is **not able** to climb it.

canoe

These two boys paddle their **canoe** so that it glides swiftly through the water.

cap

A boy wears a **cap** instead of a hat. A bottle **cap** keeps the fizz in a soda.

captain

On a ship, everybody has to obey the **captain.**
The **captain** commands the ship and decides where it is to sail.

car

Car is a nickname for an automobile.
I wish I could drive our family **car.**

card

When we go on a trip, I always send a **card** to my friend.

cardinal

The **cardinal** is a beautiful red bird that sings a pretty song.
It is also called finch or redbird.

care

Mother asked me to take **care** of my baby brother while she was talking on the telephone.

careful

We learned to be **careful** when crossing the street. We look both ways for cars.

cargo

A ship's **cargo** is the load of goods it carries.
Airplanes also carry **cargo.**

carnival

We are always happy when the **carnival** comes to town. We like the rides and the clowns.

carp

The **carp** is a fresh-water fish. Goldfish and minnows are **carps.**

carpenter

The **carpenter** is a skillful worker with wood.
He uses many tools and machines.

carpet

A **carpet** is a covering for the floor.
It may be small, or it may cover the whole room.

carrot

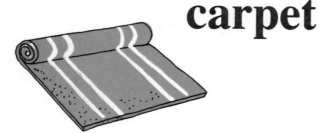

A **carrot** is an orange-colored vegetable.
Carrots taste good and are good for us.

carry

I can **carry** this big basket all by myself.

cart

It is fun to ride in the shopping **cart** at the supermarket.
Some big **carts** are pulled by horses.

carton

A **carton** is a strong box made of cardboard.
Milk and juices come in **cartons.**

carve

I **carve** a face from soft wood.
Daddy **carves** the Thanksgiving turkey and serves us all.

castle

Long ago a **castle** was the home of a rich person or a ruler.
Castles had high walls to keep enemies out.

cat

A **cat** is a very good pet.
Susan's **cat** purrs when she holds it in her lap and strokes it.

catch

I throw the ball high in the air and try to **catch** it.
My brothers play **catch** by throwing a ball back and forth between them.

caterpillar

The **caterpillar** looks like a fuzzy worm.
It will make a cocoon to sleep in.
Later it will come out as a butterfly.

cathedral

A **cathedral** is a large church.
This **cathedral** has a tall steeple.

cave

A **cave** is a hole in the earth or in the side of a mountain.
People like to explore large **caves** called **caverns.**

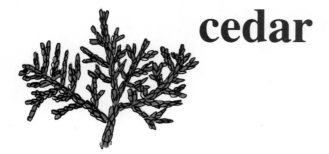

cedar

This is a branch of a **cedar** tree.
Cedars are evergreen trees.

cellar

The **cellar** under our house is dark and cool.
Mother uses it to store apples and potatoes.

cement

Cement is a white powder that comes in bags.
We mix it with water and sand or gravel to make concrete and build walls or sidewalks.

cent

A **cent** is the smallest coin in American money.
It is also called a **penny.**

center

The **center** is the middle of something.
The **center** of a target is called the bull's-eye.

certain

I am **certain** that my homework answers are right.
I am **sure** that they are right.

chair

This **chair** goes with my desk.
It is the right size for me.
Chairs in the living room are soft
and covered with cloth.

chalk

Our teacher writes on the blackboard
with a piece of **chalk**.
Sometimes we draw hopscotch lines
with **chalk.**

change

My dress is dirty.
I am going to **change** into a
clean one.
Mother calls the coins in her
purse her spare **change.**

chat

It is great fun when our family all sit
down together to have a **chat.**
We **talk** about lots of things.

cheap

This toy does not cost much
money.
It is very **cheap.**

cheek

The two sides of my face are called my **cheeks**.
Daddy says I have rosy **cheeks**.

cheese

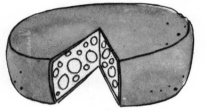

This **cheese** with big holes is called **Swiss cheese**.
Some kinds of **cheese** are soft, like **cottage cheese** or **cream cheese.**

cherry

A **cherry** is a small, sweet fruit. It makes good pies.
Cherry is a bright red color. It is named for the fruit.

chest

This **chest** has three drawers to hold my clothes.
A toy **chest** is like a deep box with a lid.

chestnut

The **chestnut** tree has beautiful flowers that look like candles.
Chestnuts are good to eat hot or in turkey stuffing.

chew

We **chew** our food with our teeth to make it small enough to swallow. Some children like to **chew** gum and blow bubbles with it.

chicken

This is a **chicken** with baby chicks.
Chickens lay eggs that we like to eat.

child

This is a little **child.** She is just learning to walk.
Soon she will learn to talk.

chilly

In the evening the air becomes **chilly.**
It is just a little bit **cold.**

china

This cup and saucer are made of **china.**
China is made of baked clay.
It comes in many colors and with beautiful designs.

Chinese

Chinese is the name of the people who live in China. It is also the name of the language they speak.

chipmunk

A **chipmunk** is a small animal like a squirrel. It is reddish brown in color, with white stripes.

chips

Chips are little pieces of anything. I love to eat **chocolate chip** cookies.

chisel

The carpenter uses the **chisel** to cut away parts of wood.
The **chisel** is also used to carve stone.

chocolate

This **chocolate** bar is big enough for the whole family.
I like dark **chocolate.**
My brother likes **milk chocolate,** and my sister likes it with almonds.

choose

Mother said I could **choose** my new dress.
I can **pick out** the one I want to buy.

Christmas

Christmas comes in December.
We are allowed to help trim the **Christmas tree.**

church

Churches look different in some countries.
What does the **church** near your home look like?

cinder

I think I have a **cinder** in my eye.
It is a little bit of ash that blew in the air.

circle

We join hands and stand in a **circle** to play some games.

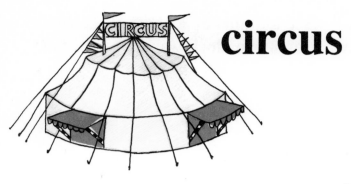

circus

In our town the **circus** is in a huge tent.
Inside, the clowns and the acrobats and the animal acts perform.

city

Jack lives in a **city** with tall buildings and wide streets. Jill lives in the country with trees and fields.

class

My **class** at school has ten children. We all study the same things.

claw

A **claw** is the sharp nail of a bird or animal.
My cat sharpens his **claws** by scratching trees.

clean

Your shoes are not **clean.** You must get the mud off and then shine them.

clear

The sky is **clear** today. There are no clouds to make it dark.

climb

My uncle has apple trees in his orchard. He lets me **climb** them.

clock

We tell time by looking at the **clock.**
An **alarm clock** wakes us by a loud
bell.

close

My best friend lives **close** to me.
She lives **near** me.

closet

In my bedroom is a **closet** built into
the wall.
I keep my clothes in this **closet.**

cloth

Girls' dresses and boys' jeans are
made of **cloth.**
The **cloth** may be wool, or cotton, or
linen.

cloud

White **clouds** sailing in the sky are a
pretty sight to see.

clover

Clover is a plant with three little
leaves.
A four-leaf **clover** is said to bring
good luck.

clown

The **clown** is a circus performer. He tumbles and does tricks to make us laugh.

coal

Coal is dug from the ground by miners. **Coal** is a fuel that we use to make heat.

coast

On the **coast** the land and the sea come together.
In winter we **coast** downhill on our sleds.

coat

Mother bought me a new winter **coat.** It has a cozy, warm lining on the inside.

cocoa

I often drink **cocoa** in the morning instead of milk.
Cocoa is a powder that is cooked with milk and sugar.

coconut

The **coconut** has a hard shell. Inside is **coconut** milk and the white flesh of the nut.

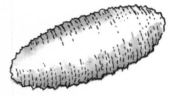

cocoon

Silk is made from the **cocoon** of the silkworm.

cod

The **cod** is a large fish that is eaten by people in many parts of the world.

coffee

This is a branch of a **coffee tree.** The drink called **coffee** is made from the seeds.

coin

A **coin** is a metal disk used as money. Our **coins** are pennies, nickels, dimes, and quarters.

cold

It is very **cold** today.
Father says the temperature is below zero.

cold

This little girl has a **cold.**

collar

My best dress has a fancy **collar** at the neck.
My dog wears a leather **collar** with his name on it.

collect

I **collect** stamps. This is my stamp album.

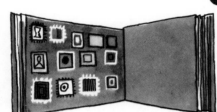

collie

A **collie** is a very clever dog. Some **collies** help farmers look after their sheep.

color

Red, yellow, blue, green, and purple are **colors.**
Yellow is the **color** I like best.

colt

A **colt** is a baby horse.
Colts can stand up and walk the same day they are born.

comb

A **comb** helps us keep our hair neat and smooth.

come

Mother says, "**Come** here." She wants me to go to her.
Daddy says, "**Come** with me." He wants me to go where he is going.

comet

A **comet** is a bright heavenly body. It looks like a star with a tail.

cone

This is the **cone** of a fir tree.
Cones hold the seeds of evergreen trees.

cook

The man with the big white hat is a **cook.**
We **cook** food with heat to make it good to eat.

cool

This is a **cool** day. It is not hot and it is not cold.

copper

Pennies are made of **copper.**
Copper is a brownish metal. It is also used to make wire.

copy

I can learn to write letters if I **copy** them from a book. I **draw** them just as they look.

cork

My father brought home a bottle that was closed with a **cork.**
We had to open it with a **corkscrew.**

corn

These are ears of **corn.**
Corn is a yellow grain.

corner

Two lines or surfaces meet at a **corner**.

correct

The teacher will **correct** my homework. She will tell me if it is done right.

cost

My book **cost** the same as Billy's. They were both the same price.

costume

James is wearing a **costume**. He is going to a **costume** party dressed as a Mexican boy.

cottage

We have a **cottage** near the seashore. It is a little house where we spend vacations.

cotton

Cotton grows in clumps called bolls. The bolls are spun into thread to make cloth.

couch

We have a large **couch** in the living room.
Three or four people can sit on the **couch.**

cough

That is a bad **cough.** Rest will help you get over your cold.

count

Count the acorns in this picture. How many are there?

couple

I have a girl-doll and a boy-doll. Everyone says they are a pretty **couple.**

cousin

My **cousin** Mary is my aunt's daughter.
My **cousin** Tom is my uncle's son.

cover

I am making a paper **cover** for my new book.
It will protect the book **cover** and keep it clean.

cow

The **cow** gives us milk. From milk we can make butter, cheese, cream, and ice cream.

crack

This wall must be very old. It has a big **crack** in it.

cracker

I like to eat a graham **cracker** with my milk.
I also like the little round **crackers** we put in soup.

cradle

The **cradle** is the baby's first bed.
Some **cradles** are on rockers so we can rock the baby to sleep.

crawl

The baby learns to **crawl** on his hands and knees before he can walk.

crayon

This **crayon** is made of wax. I draw pictures with **crayons** of many colors.

cream

Cream is the thickest part of milk. **Whipped cream** is fine to eat with strawberries.

creep

Let us **creep** under the bush. Nobody will be able to find us there.

crib

Our new baby sleeps in a **crib.** The **crib** has railings around it so that the baby will not fall out.

cricket

The **cricket** is a little insect. We hear it chirping on summer nights.

crocodile

A **crocodile** looks like a very large lizard. **Crocodiles** live in rivers and swamps.

crocus

The **crocus** is the first spring flower.
Sometimes you can see **crocuses** peeping above the late snow.

crooked

This picture is hanging **crooked.** It needs to be made straight.

cross

This church has a **cross** on top of the steeple.

cross

I am allowed to **cross** the street alone.
I go from one side to the other.

crow

This large black bird is a **crow**. **Crows** fly in flocks and make loud cawing noises.

crumbs

Sometimes I break bread into little **crumbs** and feed them to the birds.

crust

The outside of bread is the **crust**. I like the **crust**. Some people cut it off.

crutch

This boy has injured his leg. He needs a **crutch** to help him walk.

cry

I **cry** when I hurt myself. Tears come to my eyes.

cucumber

The **cucumber** grows on a low vine. **Cucumbers** are good to eat cut up in a salad.

cup

Mother is drinking from a **cup.** It has a handle to make it easy to hold.

cure

When I am sick the doctor gives me medicine to **cure** me. The medicine makes me well again.

curl

A **curl** is a little ring of hair. Some girls wear their hair in **curls** down to their shoulders.

curtain

A **curtain** covers the window. It makes the room look bright and gay.

cut

Judith knows how to **cut** a loaf of bread. She is old enough to help Mother now.

 **Dd**

dachshund

Our **dachshund** is named Fritz.
He has a long body and short legs.

dad

Dad is a nickname for father.
My **dad** is playing Ping Pong with me.

dagger

A **dagger** is a short weapon.
Daggers were used by fighting men many years ago.

daily

The sun comes up **daily.** The sun comes up **every day.**

dairy

Trucks carry milk to the **dairy** in large cans.
At the **dairy** the milk is put into cartons and bottles.

daisy

The **daisy** is a yellow and white flower.
Daisies grow wild in the fields. They are also sold in florist shops.

dam

A strong high wall holds back the water in this valley. It is a **dam.**

damp

It is not raining, but the air is **damp.**
The air still feels **wet.**

dance

I am learning to **dance.**
Sometimes we **dance** in costumes.

dandelion

A **dandelion** is one of the early spring flowers.
Dandelions look nice in fields, but Daddy does not like them in the lawn.

dare

Do not **dare** to cross the street when the light is red.
Do not take that chance of being hurt.

dark

When the sun goes down, the sky becomes **dark.**
It is then nighttime.

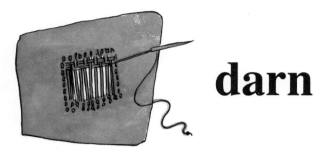

darn

I have a hole in my sleeve.
Mother will **darn** it for me.

date

The skin of the **date** is brown and shiny. The stone is long and thin. **Dates** are good to eat.

date

We can find the **date** on the calendar. It tells us the day of the week and the month of the year.

daughter

A girl child is the **daughter** of her parents.

day

A **day** has 24 hours.
A **day** begins at midnight and ends at midnight.

dead

Part of this branch has been broken by the wind. This part is **dead.**

dear

I love Mother very much. She is very **dear** to me.

December

December is the 12th month of the year. It is a winter month.

decide

I can't **decide** which dress to wear.
I am having a hard time choosing one.

deck

The floor of a ship is called the **deck.** Some houses have an open porch that is called a **deck.**

deep

Children are not allowed to swim here. The water is too **deep.** It is over their heads.

deer

This animal is a male **deer.** He is called a stag or a buck.

deliver

The boy is here to **deliver** the newspaper. He brings us the paper every day.

dentist

I go to the **dentist** twice a year. He cleans my teeth. If I have a hole in a tooth, he fills it.

desert

In the **desert** everything is brown and dry.
There is almost no water and not many trees in the **desert.**

deserve

When you do a good job, you **deserve** to be thanked. You have earned thanks.

desk

I sit at my **desk** in school and keep my books and pencils in it.

dessert

We are having a special **dessert** of fruit, nuts, and ice cream for dinner today.

dew

Early on a summer morning the grass has tiny sparkling drops of water on it. This is called **dew.**

dial

Sally can **dial** the telephone.
She can turn the **dial** to the numbers she wants to make a call.

diamond

The sparkling stone in this ring is a **diamond.**
If you move it about in the light, you will see the colors of the rainbow.

diaper

The baby's first clothing is a **diaper.**
The **diaper** is a kind of underwear that can be thrown away when it is soiled.

diary

I have a new **diary.** I will write in it what I have done every day.

dice

In some board games we use **dice** to tell us how far we can move.
The **dice** are small cubes with dots that stand for numbers.

dictionary

I use the **dictionary** to find the meaning of words.
This book is a **dictionary.**

different

My dress is **different** from Mary's.
It is **not the same** as Mary's.

dig   Dogs like to **dig** in the ground and bury a bone.
I like to **dig** in the sand at the seashore.

dime   Daddy gave me a **dime** to buy candies.
A **dime** can buy ten penny candies.

dinner   **Dinner** is my favorite meal. We have it in the evening when Daddy is home.

dirty   When John plays baseball he gets his clothes **dirty.** Then Mother has to wash them.

discover   I **discover** new things when I look carefully.
Today I **discovered** a bird's nest.

dishes   Our **dishes** are kept in a kitchen cabinet. When I set the table, I have to take care not to drop them.

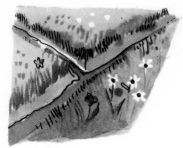

ditch

There is a **ditch** around the field near our house.
Rainwater collects in the **ditch** and makes things grow.

dive

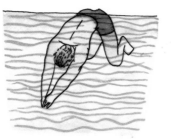

We practice **diving** at the swimming pool.
When I **dive,** I can stay underwater a long time.

divide

Jerry will **divide** his candy among his friends.
He will separate it into pieces for each one.

doctor

The **doctor** knows all about how our bodies work.
He can tell when we are sick.
He knows how to make us well.

dog

A **dog** is an animal.
Dogs make good pets. They come in all shapes and sizes and colors.

dollar

A **dollar** is a piece of paper money. It is worth 100 pennies or 10 dimes or four quarters.

donkey

Weekends I often go to the park near our house.
A man who keeps a **donkey** there gives me a ride.

door

We go in and out of our house through the **door.**
We open the **door** to go out and close it behind us.

dot

A **dot** is a small spot.
Today I am wearing my white blouse with red polka **dots.**

double

This is a **double** boiler.
It is used for cooking.
A **double** boiler has two pots.
One pot fits into the other.

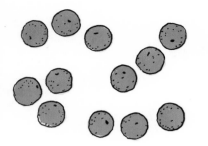

dozen

At the supermarket you will see large piles of oranges. They are packed in bags of a **dozen**.
There are **12** in each bag.

drain

The **drain** in the sink lets the water run out.
The stopper in the **drain** keeps the water in.

drawing

Allen is making a **drawing** of a house. It is a good **picture.**

dream

Last night I had an exciting **dream** while I slept.
I **dreamed** that our family went on a trip together.

dress

I wore my new **dress** for the first time today.
I chose the pattern for it myself.

drink

I **drink** milk with my meals.
Sometimes I **drink** fruit juice.

drip

The water **drips** from the faucet if it is not shut tight.
The rain **drips** from the edges of the roof.

drive

My brother is learning to **drive** the car.
Daddy is teaching him to make it run.

drop

The faucet of the kitchen sink is dripping.
The water is falling **drop** by **drop.**

drop

When I set the table I am careful not to **drop** the dishes. I do not **let them fall** and break.

druggist

When the doctor wants us to have medicine, the **druggist** mixes the medicine for us and tells us how much to take.

drum

Jim has a new **drum.**
He is beating the **drum** with his fingers.

dry

It is a fine day and a good breeze is blowing.
The clothes will soon be **dry.**

duck

A **duck** is a water bird.
These **ducks** are white. Other **ducks** have brightly colored feathers.

dwarf

A **dwarf** is a very small grownup.
In fairy tales a **dwarf** is sometimes shown like this.

E e

each

Each of the children takes a turn.
Every one of the children takes a turn.

eager

Mary was **eager** to go with her father.
Mary **wanted very much** to go with her father.

eagle

The **eagle** is called the king of the birds.
Eagles live among the high mountains.

ear

Hold the clock close to your **ear.** Now you can hear it ticking very easily.

ear

This is another kind of **ear.**
Ears like this grow on cereal plants like corn.

early

I have breakfast **early** in the morning.
I have breakfast at the beginning of
the morning.

earn

Daddy goes to work to **earn** money for
his family.
He **is paid** for the time he spends at
the office.

earrings

Rosita is a little Spanish girl.
She and many of her friends
wear **earrings.**

earth

The **earth** in the flowerpot is soft
and loose.
The gardener mixed it.

earth

The planet we live on is called
Earth.

east

The sun shines into my room in the
morning. My bedroom faces **east.**

Easter

Easter is a spring holiday when we wear our best clothes. Mother may give us an **Easter basket** of eggs and candies.

easy

It is **easy** to learn to ride a bicycle.
It is **not hard** to learn to ride a bicycle.

eat

We are going to **eat** now. Mother is serving the food.

echo

''Hello,'' we shout toward the woods.
A faint answer comes back: ''Hello.''
This is an **echo.**

eel

The **eel** is a fish. It looks like a snake.

effort

Daisy is making an **effort** to do well in school.
She is **trying hard.**

egg

I am having a boiled **egg** for breakfast.
Sometimes I have a **scrambled egg** or a **fried egg.**

eight

Eight is a number. It is the sum of seven and one, or six and two, or five and three, or four and four.

elbow

I can bend my arm by moving my **elbow.**

electric

In our house we have **electric** lights. When we turn on the switch, the room is lit up.

elephant

The **elephant** is one of the largest animals in the world.
He is very strong.

elevator

At the department store we rode in the **elevator.**
It carried us up and down from floor to floor.

elf

An **elf** is a tiny make-believe person. **Elves** are supposed to work in Santa's workshop.

elk

The **elk** is a large deer with horns called antlers.

elm

The **elm** tree gives lovely shade in the summer.
Elm wood is hard.
Carpenters like to build with it.

else

I do not want to play hopscotch. I would rather play something **else.**

empty

I drank all my milk. The glass is **empty.**

end

We rode the bus to the **end** of the line.
We went to the last stop.

engine

The **engine** of this modern train is driven by oil.
It is a **diesel engine.**

English

In the United States and Canada, we speak **English.**
It is our language.

enter

When I **enter** the classroom, I sit at my desk.
When I **go into** the classroom, I sit at my desk.

entire

We stayed at the beach the **entire** afternoon.
We stayed at the beach the **whole** afternoon.

envelope

I received a birthday card in an **envelope.**
The **envelope** had my name and address and a stamp on it.

equal

Let's divide the candy into **equal** pieces.
Let's divide the candy into pieces of the **same size.**

eraser

My pencil has an **eraser** at the top.
I rub out mistakes with the **eraser.**

errand

Mother asked me to run an **errand** for her.
She asked me to go to the store for her.

error

Mary did her arithmetic without a single **error.**
She didn't make any **mistake.**

escalator

In the department store, I like to ride the **escalator.**
The **moving stairs** take us to the different floors.

Eskimo

The **Eskimo** lives in the far North.
In the winter **Eskimos** live in igloos made of snow.

evening

This is an **evening** in the fall.
The darkness has come early.

evergreen

Fir trees are **evergreens.**
They do not shed their
leaves in the winter.

every

I brush my teeth **every** morning.
I brush my teeth **each** morning.

everybody

Everybody in our class
passed the test.
Every person in our
class passed the test.

everything

We have **everything**
we need to make a pie.
We have **all the things**
we need to make a pie.

except

Everyone **except** Jean went swimming.
Everyone **but** Jean went swimming.

exchange

Harry and I are going to **exchange** stamps. I have some that he does not have.

excuse

Barbara said, "Please **excuse** me for bumping you."
She wanted her friend to forgive her.

exercise

Riding a bicycle is good **exercise.** It helps to make your body strong.

eye

Jane points to her **eye.**
Wherever we look, we see things with our **eyes.**

 **F f**

face

I know how to draw a **face.** I put in the eyes and the nose and the mouth.

factory

A **factory** is a large building where things are made.

fairy

A **fairy** is a make-believe creature. Tinkerbell is the **fairy** in the story Peter Pan.

fall

The leaves on the trees are red, brown, and gold.
It is the beginning of **fall.**

false

Virginia told a **false** story.
The story was **not true.**

family

This is our **family:** Father, Mother, Richard, and me.

far

Our home is **far** from the ocean.
It is a **long way** from the ocean.

fare

Daddy pays the **fare** when we ride on the bus.
He gives the driver money to let us ride.

farm

In the summer I stay with Uncle George on his **farm.**
He grows vegetables and keeps cattle, pigs, and chickens.

farmer

When Grandfather was a boy, the **farmer** had to harness a horse to his plow.

fast

Hurry up and you will see the **fast** new car. It has just raced around the corner.

fat   If I eat too much, I will become **fat.**
I will be too heavy.

father   My **father** is one of my parents.
My mother is my other parent.

fear   **Fear** of falling makes me climb carefully.
Being afraid of falling makes me climb carefully.

feather   Birds have **feathers** to keep them warm.
I made an Indian headdress from many colored **feathers.**

February   **February** is the second month of the year.
It is usually snowy and cold in **February.**

feel   In blindman's buff we **feel** our way around.
We **touch** the players around us.

feet

I have two **feet** to walk with. My dog has four **feet.**
How many **feet** is it to that tree?

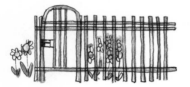 

fence

Uncle George has put up a **fence.** The **fence** will keep the farm animals out of the flower garden.

fern

Many kinds of **fern** grow in different parts of the world. They are found in damp, shady places.

ferry

Susy loves to ride on the **ferry.** The big boat carries people and cars across the river.

fever

Irene has to stay in bed. She has a **fever.**
Her body is too hot because she is sick.

few

I keep a **few** pencils in my desk. I like to have more than one.

field

This **field** is full of golden wheat.
In other **fields** farmers grow vegetables
or grass to feed the cattle.

figure

On the watch face we can see
eleven **figures.**
The **figure** 6 is covered up.

file

The key does not fit the lock well. Father
must **file** it down a little at the end.

fill

I could not find a funnel. So I had to **fill** the
bottles very carefully.

film

We saw an interesting **film** at school. It
was a **movie** about the sea.

find   This is a picture puzzle. Can you **find** the hidden animals? Can you see the hidden animals?

fine   Betsy is doing **fine** work in school.
Betsy is doing **very good** work in school.
Mother is sewing a **fine** seam.
Mother is sewing with very small stitches.

finger   My hand has four **fingers** and a thumb.

finish   You must **finish** your supper before you play.
You must eat all of your supper before you play.
The **finish line** is the end of the race.

fire   This house is on **fire.** It is burning.
The firemen are trying to put out the **fire.**

fire alarm

This is a **fire alarm.**
If we see a building on
fire, we break the little
window in the **fire
alarm** and push the
button inside.

firefly

The **firefly** is a beetle that makes its
own light.
Fireflies make the garden glow on
summer evenings.

fireworks

The **fireworks** shoot up in
the air and burst into
sparks of light.

first

Lucy is **first** in line. She is before
everyone else.
The crocus is the **first** flower of spring.
It blooms before the other flowers.

fish

Fish are animals that live in water.
Jack is fishing and has caught his third
fish.

fit   This suit is a good **fit.** It is just the right size.

five   **Five** is a number. It is the sum of four and one, or three and two.

fix   My bicycle is broken. I will ask Daddy to **fix** it.

flag   The Red Cross **flag** is known in all countries.
It stands for helping people in trouble.

flake This **flake** of snow has a very special shape.
No two **snowflakes** are exactly alike.

flame The **flame** of the candle burns brightly in the darkness.

float

Ben can **float** in the water. He lies on top of the water without swimming.

flock

The shepherd and the dog are watching the **flock** of sheep.
They want to keep the sheep together.

flood

A **flood** covered the land when the dam broke and let the water out.

floor

The **floor** is the part of a building that we walk on.
A big building may have many **floors.**

flour

Flour is a fine powder made from wheat or rye.

flower

This **flower** grows in our garden.
Most **flowers** are brightly colored.

fly

The **fly** is a small insect with two wings. **Flies** can carry sicknesses, so we try to keep them out of our houses.

flying fish

The **flying fish** lives in warm seas. When it leaps through the air it looks as if it could fly.

fog

Fog is tiny droplets of water hanging in the air.
It is hard to see or to drive in **fog.**

follow

We like to play **follow** the leader. All of us go behind the first one in line.

food

To be strong, we should always eat the right kinds of **food.**

foot

I can hop on one **foot.** I know many hopping games.

football

Football is an exciting game. Sometimes the players all pile up in a heap on top of the **football.**

forehead

My **forehead** is the part of my face between my eyes and my hair.

forest

The **forest** is a cool and quiet place. The tall trees are full of small animals.

forget

Betty had better not **forget** to take her umbrella with her. It looks like rain.

forgive

By accident, I gave Grandmother a push. I told her I was sorry, and I hope she will **forgive** me.

fork

I can eat with a **fork** now, too. When I was smaller I could only eat with a spoon.

fort

This is an old **fort.** It was built by people many years ago to protect them from attack.

fountain

In our park there is a big **fountain.**
When it is windy, the water sprays around the **fountain.**

four

Four is a number. It is the sum of three and one, or two and two.

fox

A **fox** is a wild animal with long fur and a bushy tail.
The **fox** belongs to the dog family.

fraction

Three fourths (¾) is a
fraction.
A **fraction** is a part of
anything.

frame

This gray **frame** goes well with the
colors of the picture.

freeze

If it is very cold, the water in the
pond will **freeze.**
The water will become hard.
Frozen water is ice.

fresh

Vegetables just picked from the
garden are **fresh.**
Last night we had a **fresh** fall of
snow.
Michael was **fresh** to his teacher. He
was impolite.

Friday

Friday is a day of the week.
Friday comes between Thursday
and Saturday.

friend

Tom is my **friend.** He is a person I like.

frighten

We must be quiet and not **frighten** the birds.
We do not want to **scare** them away.

frog

A **frog** is a small animal with strong hind legs.
A **frog** can jump very far.
Frogs make a loud noise called croaking.

frost

After a cold, damp night, the dew and the dampness freeze and make **frost.**

fruit

Fruit is the part of a plant or tree that holds the seeds.
Apples, pears, plums, and cherries are **fruit.**

full

Mother says, "Don't talk with your mouth **full**."
She means, "Don't speak with food in your mouth."

fun

A picnic is **fun**. It is **enjoyable**.

funnel

A **funnel** is a tool that helps us to pour into a bottle with a small mouth.

fur

Mother's special present for Christmas was a **fur** coat.

furnace

Our house is heated by a **furnace**.
A **furnace** burns oil or gas or coal to make heat.

furniture

Danny's father bought new **furniture**.
He bought a couch, a table, an armchair, and a bookcase.

G g

gallon

A **gallon** is an amount of a liquid. A **gallon** is more than a quart or a pint.

gallop

This horse is running at a **gallop.** It goes fast and lifts all four feet off the ground once in each stride.

game

Hopscotch is a **game.** Football is a **game.**
Bridge is a card **game.**
Both children and grownups play **games** to have fun.

garage

Our neighbors built a **garage** next to their house.
Now they need not keep their car in the street.

garden

Our **garden** has both grass and flowers.
Some **gardens** are planted with vegetables.

gate

The gatekeeper is in charge of the factory **gate.**
He opens it to let people drive in.

gather

Mother is going to **gather** fresh corn for dinner.
She is going to **pick** the corn from the garden.
The boys **gather** in the yard for a ballgame. The boys **come together** to play a game.

gay

Today I feel **gay** and cheerful. I want to sing all the time.

gem

A **gem** is a beautiful stone used in jewelry.

gentian

Gentian is a kind of flower that comes in different shapes and colors.
This is a fringed **gentian.**

gentle

I am always **gentle** with my kitten.
I am never rough or harsh.

German shepherd

The **German shepherd** is a large, strong dog.
It is sometimes called police dog.

giant

I read a fairy tale about a huge **giant** in my storybook.

gift

I have bought a Christmas **gift** for my brother.
I will wrap it and put it under the tree.

giraffe

The tallest animal in the zoo is the **giraffe.**
The **giraffe** has a long neck and a spotted coat.

girl

I am a **girl.** My sister Angela is a **girl** too.

give

Joan is going to **give** her friend her favorite book.
She is going to let her friend keep the book.

glasses

When Father drives the car, he puts on his **glasses.**

globe

This is my **globe.**
It looks like the earth. Maps of all the countries of the world are shown on it.

gloves

It is very cold today. I shall put on my **gloves** when I go outdoors.

glue

We use **glue** to stick things together.
My brother uses a special **glue** to make his model airplanes.

gnaw

These are the four teeth that rodents use to **gnaw.**

Rats, squirrels, rabbits, and beavers bite with long, sharp teeth like these.

go

We **go** for a walk in the park.

When we **go,** we move from one place to another.

goat

Here is a mother **goat** with her frisky little kid.

Some **goats** live in the mountains and leap from rock to rock.

gold

These are two rings made of **gold.**

Gold is a shiny yellow metal.

Gold is also a name for the color yellow.

goldfish

My friend David has an aquarium with **goldfish** in it.

gong

We have a big **gong** hanging in our hall.
When you strike it with a mallet, it sounds like a bell.

goose

The **goose** is waddling to the pond with its goslings.
It is going to look for food in the water.

gorilla

The **gorilla** is the largest and strongest of the apes.
When he stands on his feet, he is taller than most men.

grade

Nancy is in the second **grade.**
Our school has eight **grades.**

grain

Grain is an important food.
This picture shows several kinds of **grain:** oats, rye, barley, wheat, corn, and rice.

grandfather

The children go for a walk with their **grandfather.** He is the father of their father or their mother.

grape

A **grape** is a small round fruit that grows in bunches.
Grapes grow on vines. They are green, red, purple, or black.

grass

Green **grass** grows in fields and lawns.
When **grass** becomes tall, the seeds grow on thin stems.

grasshopper

Look at the **grasshopper.** It is sitting on a blade of grass.

grate

I cannot make a cake by myself, but I can **grate** the lemon peel. I scrape it on the grater to make tiny pieces.

gravel

We put **gravel** on the front walk.
Now, when it rains the walk will
not be muddy.

gray

Gray is a soft color made by mixing
black and white.
When the sky is covered with clouds,
it becomes **gray** instead of blue.

great

George Washington was a **great**
man. He was a very **important** man.
The redwood is a **great** tree. It is the
largest tree in the world.

greedy

Vicky is a **greedy** child. She eats
too much.

green

Green is the color of most plants.
The grass, the new leaves of the
apple tree, and the needles of the
pine are different shades of **green.**

greyhound

A **greyhound** is a tall
thin dog.
Greyhounds can run
very fast.

grin

Jerry gave a big **grin** when he saw his new sled.
He **smiled** very widely with happiness.

grocer

We are talking to the **grocer.** He is selling us some food in his grocery store.

ground

The farmer plows the **ground** on his tractor.
He makes the **soil** soft and loose so that seeds will grow.

grow

All living things **grow.** This little boy is getting larger so fast that his pants are too short for him.

guess

Guess how wide our house is. How wide do you think it is?

guest

We have a **guest** this evening. Daddy has invited a friend to come to visit.

guide

The Forest Ranger will **guide** us through the hills.
He will **show us the way to go.**

guitar

The **guitar** is a musical instrument.
It is played by plucking the strings.

gull

The **gull** is a sea bird.
Gulls fly over the water and dive in to catch fish.

gun

This **gun** is a rifle.
When a hunter goes hunting, he slings his **gun** over his shoulder.

 **H h**

hail

The **hail** is drumming on the window. The **hail** is tiny bits of ice that fall like rain.

hair

Nancy has a doll with real **hair.** She can braid the **hair** and then comb it out.

half

This apple has been cut in **half.**
It is in **two parts.**

hall

In this large **hall** the seats are arranged in rows.
Our school auditorium is a kind of **hall.**

hammer

Bruce is nailing a box together with a **hammer.**
He is using a claw **hammer.**
If he hits a nail wrong, he can pull it out with the claw.

hand

My **hand** has five fingers. The short finger is the thumb.

hang

This animal **hangs** upside down from trees.
I **hang** pictures on the walls of my room.
At school, we all **hang** our coats in the coat closet.

happy

We are **happy** when Daddy comes home from a trip.
We are **glad** to see him.

harbor

Ships in a **harbor** are protected from the sea.
They are made fast to the **harbor wall.**

hard

This arithmetic problem is **hard** to do.
It is **not easy.**
My new bed is very **hard.** It is **not soft.**

harp

A **harp** is a musical instrument with long and short strings.
When the strings are plucked, they make a fine sound.

harvest

When the crops are ripe, the **harvest** begins.
The farmer cuts the plants and gets them ready to use.

hat

It is windy out today. I shall wear a **hat** to keep my head warm and my hair neat.

hawk

This is a **hawk** gliding through the air. It soars without moving its wings.

hay

The grass has been cut and has dried. Now it is **hay** and is loaded on the **hay** wagons.

head

This is my **head.**
All animals have a **head** with eyes, ears, a nose, and a mouth.

hear

The ear is the part of the body used for hearing.
Are your ears as good as mine? I can **hear** very well.

heart

My **heart** pumps the blood all through my body.
When I am excited, I can feel my **heart** beat.

heat

The stove is hot. Its **heat** is warming the room.

heavy

I am carrying the baby in my arms. I can carry him easily. He is not **heavy.**

hedge

We have a **hedge** around our yard. It is made of bushes planted very close together.

heel

My foot has the toes in front and the **heel** at the back.

helicopter

This is a **helicopter.** It has a propeller on top to lift it from the ground.

help

We like to **help** this old lady. We **make things easier** for her.

hem

I have grown too tall for my dress. Mother is going to let down the **hem** to make it longer.

hemlock

The **hemlock** is a tall evergreen tree. Its wood is good for making paper.

hen

The **hen** is a mother chicken.
The **hen** lays eggs and takes care of the chicks when they hatch.

herring

The **herring** is a small fish. It lives in the northern oceans.

high

In the big city the buildings are very **high**.
They are so **tall** it is hard to see their tops.

highway

This is a modern **highway**. Several lanes of traffic run side by side in both directions.

hike

We went on a **hike** in the woods.
We took a lunch to eat during our **long walk**.

hill
I can see a long way from the top of the **hill.**
The land is higher there.

hippopotamus
This is the **hippopotamus** at our zoo.
He lives mostly in the water.

hockey
Ice **hockey** is a fast game played on skates. It is a popular winter sport.

hoe
John is helping Daddy in the garden. He uses a **hoe** to dig weeds out of the flower beds.

hole
My dog has dug a **hole** in the ground. He will bury a bone in the **empty** space.

hollow
A rubber ball is **hollow.** It has an **empty space** inside.

holly

At Christmas, **holly** branches make our homes look festive with their shiny green leaves and red berries.

home

This is our **home.** It is where our family lives.

honest

Parents teach children to be **honest.**
They teach them not to tell lies or steal.

honey

This morning we are having **honey** on our toast.
The **honey** was made by bees and gathered by the beekeeper.

hook

Father will hammer the yellow **hook** into the wall.
Then he will hang a picture on it.

hoop

I have a colored **hoop.** I can roll the **hoop** a long way without letting it fall.

hop

When we play hopscotch, we **hop** from one square to the next on one foot.

horn

The deer has large **horns** growing out of his head.

horse

The **horse** is a useful animal. We can ride on it.
We can have it pull a farm wagon.
We can watch horses prance in a parade.

hose

It has not rained for a long time. Harry has brought out the **hose** to water the lawn.

hot

Be careful. The kettle is boiling. It is very **hot.**

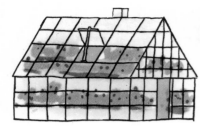

hothouse

This **hothouse** is built of glass so that the plants can receive sunlight but also be kept warm.
A **hothouse** is also called a greenhouse.

hour

Sixty minutes make an **hour.**
You can see the **hour hand,** the minute hand, and the second hand on this clock.

house

This **house** is where Ann lives.
The **house** has many rooms. It has a living room, bedrooms, and a kitchen.

hug

When Daddy comes home, he gives me a big **hug.**
He wraps his arms around me and squeezes.

hummingbird

This tiny **hummingbird** is as brightly colored as a butterfly.

hunt
In the fall some people go hunting. They **hunt** deer and ducks and other animals.

hurry
We must **hurry,** or we'll be late for school.
We must **move quickly.**

hurt
If you bump your head, it will **hurt.** It will cause you **pain.**

hush
Mother sang a lullaby to **hush** the baby. The song made the baby be **quiet.**

hyacinth
The **hyacinth** is a bell-shaped spring flower. It smells very good and has lovely colors.

I i

ice

In winter the water in the lake freezes into **ice** and we go **ice-skating.**

iceberg

An **iceberg** is a huge block of ice in the ocean.
Ships have to watch out for **icebergs,** because only the tip of the ice shows above the water.

icebreaker

In winter, parts of the sea and some rivers freeze solid.
An **icebreaker** is a ship that opens channels for other ships to sail through.

icicle

An **icicle** is formed from dripping water that freezes.
Icicles are all around the roof of this house.

igloo

An Eskimo builds his **igloo** out of blocks of snow.
He and his family use the **igloo** as their home.

ill   Mary is feeling **ill** today. She feels too **sick** to go to school.

immediately   Mother told us to start our homework **immediately.** She told us to begin **right away.**

improve   Jill is trying to **improve** her handwriting. She is trying to **make** her handwriting **better.**

Indian   This **Indian** is wearing his native costume. **Indians** were the first people to live in North America.

ink   I write with **ink** now. I can write neatly without spilling the **ink.**

insect   Flies, bees, ants, and butterflies all belong to the **insect** family.

invite

I am sending an invitation to my friends. I want to **invite** them to my birthday party.

iris

The **iris** is a large flower that may be purple or yellow.
Several **irises** grow on one stem.

iron

This garden gate is made of **iron.**
Iron is a strong, useful metal.

island

An **island** is a piece of land with water all around it.
An **island** may be very small, or it may be as large as Greenland.

ivy

Ivy is a climbing plant.
You can see the tiny shoots that help it cling to a tree or a wall.

125

J j

jam

Mother makes fruit **jam.** She cooks peaches or plums with sugar to make a delicious spread for bread.

January

January is the first month of the year.
New Year's Day is the first day of **January.**

jar

A **jar** is a glass container with a wide mouth.
We buy mayonnaise and pickles in **jars.**

jaw

The **jaws** are the part of your face that hold the teeth.
The lower **jaw** moves up and down when you chew.

jeans

Mary Ann wore her new **jeans** to school today.
Both boys and girls like these strong cotton **pants.**

jellyfish

A **jellyfish** is a sea animal. A **jellyfish** floating in the water looks like a lump of jelly.

job Jimmy got a **job** delivering papers after school. He works every day and is paid money.

join Joe is going to **join** the Boy Scouts. He is going to **become a member** of the Boy Scouts.

joint A **joint** is the part of the body where two bones move on each other. The elbow is a **joint** in your arm.

joke We are laughing at a **joke** we heard. It was a very **funny story.**

judge A **judge** is a man who settles quarrels. He usually wears robes like these.

jug This **jug** is a fat pitcher. We use it to serve milk at the table.

juice

This pear is full of **juice.** When I bite it, the **juice** runs down my chin.

July

July is the seventh month of the year. In our part of the country **July** is usually very hot.

jump

The other day we saw a film about skiing. It showed how skiers **jump.**

June

June is the sixth month of the year. The weather is usually beautiful and warm in **June.**

jungle

The **jungle** is a huge **forest.** It is the home of many animals but very few people.

K k  kangaroo

The **kangaroo** has strong hind legs.
It does not run; it jumps.
The mother **kangaroo** carries her baby in a pouch on her stomach.

kayak

Uncle Bill has a **kayak.**
A **kayak** is an Eskimo **canoe** that holds one person and is all covered on top.

key

A **key** opens the lock on a door.
Mother keeps her **keys** on a keyring.

kick

The football player can **kick** the ball a long way.
He strikes it with his foot to try to score points.

kid

A **kid** is a baby goat. **Kid** is also a nickname for a child.

king

A **king** is a ruler of a country.
Not many countries have a government with a **king** anymore.

kingfisher

The **kingfisher** is a handsome bird that feeds on fish. It lives near lakes and rivers and dives for its food.

kiss

I always want Mother to **kiss** me goodnight. She touches her lips to my face to let me know she loves me.

kitchen

Mother is in charge of the **kitchen.** She does all of the cooking there.

kite

We made a **kite** to fly in the air. We put a funny face on it.

kitten

My friend Nancy is very happy with the **kitten** we gave her. A **kitten** is a **baby cat.** It is soft and cuddly.

knee

Marion loves to "ride a cockhorse" on her father's **knee.**

knife

A **knife** is used for cutting.
Knives are made in many shapes and sizes for cutting different things.

knight

This **knight** is a soldier of olden times. He wears a suit of metal and carries a shield and a lance.

knit

Susy is learning to **knit.** She is making a scarf, using **knitting needles** to loop the yarn into fabric.

knock

There is a **knock** at the door. Someone bangs the knocker to let us know he is there.

knot

These cords are tied in a **knot.**
We can untie the **knot** or cut it apart.

ladder

The **ladder** is ready for the workman to climb to reach the top of the house.

ladybug

A **ladybug** is a pretty little beetle.
Ladybugs also help gardeners by eating the eggs of harmful insects.

lake

We are camping beside a small **lake** near the woods.
The **lake** is entirely surrounded by land.

lamb

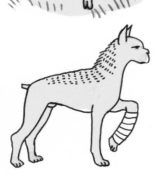

A **lamb** is a baby sheep.
Sometimes we say a friendly dog is gentle as a **lamb.**

lame

This dog has been hurt. His left foreleg is **lame,** so he cannot run very well.

lamp

A **lamp** is a stand for holding light bulbs.
Lamps usually have a shade to make the light softer.

land

The aircraft glides down lower and lower. In a moment it will **land** at the airport.

lantern

Last night we had a garden party. Mother lit **lanterns** to give light.

large

My geography book is very **large.** It is **big** enough to hold many maps.

last

Mary ate the **last** cookie. She ate the only one left.
John was the **last** boy in line. No one was behind him.

late

We must run. We might be **late** for school. We might not be there when school begins.

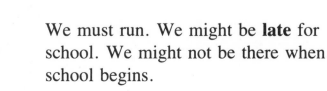

laugh

I have to **laugh** when I hear a funny story. I also **laugh** when my sister tickles me.

lawn

Kenny mows the **lawn** for his father. He cuts the grass so that it is nice and even.

lazy

My cat is very **lazy.** She doesn't run or play. She just likes to sleep by the fire.

lead

Look at our long line of girls. Today it is Helen's turn to **lead.**
She **goes first** and we all follow her.

leaf

A **leaf** is a part of a tree or plant. **Leaves** like this one fall off the tree in the winter. New ones grow in the spring.

leak

This pail has a **leak.** You can see the water coming out through a hole at the bottom.

learn

Jill wants to **learn** to write. She will **find out how** to make letters and words.

left

This is my **left** arm.
I am pointing it to the **left.**

lemon

The **lemon** is a sour fruit. **Lemon** juice with sugar and water makes lemonade.

lend

Bob has used up his allowance. His mother will **lend** him money, and he will pay it back later.

lesson

Our teacher put the **lesson** on the blackboard. She wrote down what she wanted us to learn today.

Dear John,

Thank you very much for your letter. I am glad you enjoyed staying with us. I hope you will come again next summer.

Roy

Mister John Daily
356 Main St.
Park Ridge, Ill.

letter

John found a **letter** in the mailbox. It was addressed to him.

lever

We cannot move this heavy crate without help. We must pry it up with a **lever.**

library

Our school has a big **library.** It has many books on the shelves.

lick

My cat likes to **lick** cream with his tongue. He also **licks** his fur to make it clean.

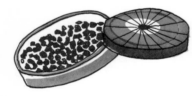

licorice

These little black candies are **licorice.** They are made from the root of a plant.

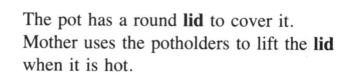

lid

The pot has a round **lid** to cover it. Mother uses the potholders to lift the **lid** when it is hot.

lie

Evelyn is ill. She has to **lie** in bed.

136

lie   I must not tell a **lie.** It is not right to say something that is **not true.**

lift   Can you **lift** the basket with one hand? It is very heavy.

light   Frank is swinging the parcel as if there were nothing in it. It must be very **light.**

light   The **light** at the top of the lighthouse goes round and round. It shines far to warn ships of danger.

lightning   Did you see that flash of **lightning?**
It jumped from one storm cloud to another.

lilac

We have two **lilac** bushes in our garden.
One has white flowers and the other
lavender flowers.
Both colors of **lilac** smell very good.

lily

A **lily** is a plant that grows from a bulb
and has large flowers.
Lilies grow in many colors.
The **Easter lily** is snow white. The **tiger
lily** is orange.

liner

The huge ocean **liner** sails all the way
across the sea.
Some **liners** take passengers on
cruises, just to have fun on board ship.

lion

The **lion** is a large wild animal of the cat
family.
The **lion** is so fierce that it is called the
"king of beasts."

lips

William is blowing air through his **lips.**
He is whistling.
He also uses his **lips** when he speaks.

listen

When we **listen** to the teacher, we
hear with our ears and pay attention
to what she is saying.

little

I have a **little** money in my piggybank. I do not have much. Mary is my **little** sister. She is smaller than I.

lizard

A **lizard** belongs to the snake family.
It has four legs and a scaly skin. It runs very fast.

llama

The **llama** looks like a camel without a hump.
The people of South America use it as a beast of burden.
They also make cloth of its wool.

lobster

The **lobster** is a sea animal. When it is caught, it is dark green.
It turns bright red when it is cooked.

lock

This kind of **lock** is used to fasten a chain.
It is called a **padlock.**

look

Dorothy and Brian are taking a **look** at a family of birds.
They are using their eyes to **see** the birds.

loud   The thunder was very **loud** last night. It made a **great noise.**

loudspeaker   This is a **loudspeaker** at the airport.
It makes voices carry a long distance.

low   The branches on a Christmas tree are very **low.**
They almost touch the ground.

lumber   Behind the sawmill, **lumber** is stored in large piles.
The **lumber** has been cut into planks for building.

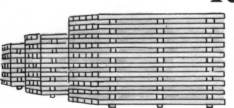

lunch   **Lunch** is one of my favorite meals.
It is the meal between breakfast and dinner.

lungs   George is breathing fresh air into his **lungs.**
His **lungs** carry oxygen from the air to his blood.

M m magazine

Bert is reading a **magazine** about his favorite sport.
Other **magazines** are about the news or business or places to visit.

magic

The magician is pulling bunches of flowers from an empty bag.
It is called **magic,** but it is really a trick.

magnet

A **magnet** is a piece of metal that can pick up things made of iron and steel.

magnolia

This beautiful white and pink flower is the blossom of the **magnolia** tree.
It is the first tree to bloom in the spring.

mail

Fred is putting a letter in the **mailbox.**
Soon the letter carrier will come by to collect all the **mail** in the box.

make

"What are you trying to **make?**" "I am making a bookmark."

mammoth

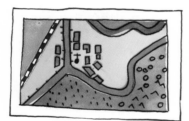

The **mammoth** was a huge elephant.
This kind was called the **woolly mammoth** because of its long fur.

many

Our school has **many** children. A **great number** of boys and girls study there.

map

This is a **map** of our neighborhood. It shows all the houses and streets as they look from an airplane.

marble

This statue is made of **marble. Marble** is a kind of stone that can be carved into a figure. It is then polished until it is shiny.

March

March is the third month of the year. It is the month when spring begins.

margarine

Margarine looks like butter. It is used in cooking and as a spread for bread.

marigold

A **marigold** is a yellow or orange flower that is grown in gardens.

market

A **market** is a place where things are sold.
There are meat **markets** and fruit **markets** and vegetable **markets.**

marry

Mother's friends Elizabeth and Norman went to church to **marry.** This is their **wedding** day.

mask

This is the **mask** I am going to wear on Halloween.
Do you think I will frighten anyone?

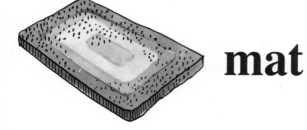

mat

The **mat** in front of our door is wearing out.
Too many people have wiped their feet on it in wet weather.

143

match

We use a **match** to light a fire. We have to be very careful not to burn ourselves.

May

May is the fifth month of the year. It is a month full of flowers and spring breezes.

mayor

This is the **mayor** of our town. He is the head of the city government.

meat

Mother bought **meat** at the butcher's. She bought a roast of beef, some pork chops, and some lamb for stew.

mechanic

A **mechanic** does many different jobs with tools and machines.
He wears overalls for his work.

medicine

Catherine is ill. She has to take a spoonful of **medicine** every three hours to help her get well.

meeting

This evening there is a
meeting at the town hall.
Many people are going there
to hear a speech.

melt

When the sun comes out the snow will
melt. It will **thaw,** or **turn to water**
again.

memory

Mother has a very good
memory. She remembers
things that happened when
she was a little girl.

merry-go-round

The **merry- go- round** in
the park has both horses and
cars. I like to ride the
horses best.

mess

My room is a **mess.**
I must pick up my toys and put them
away.

milk

Children need fresh **milk** every day. It helps to make their teeth and bones strong.

mill

Grain is ground in a **mill** to make flour.
This **mill** is called a **windmill.**
The wind makes the machinery turn.

minister

On Sunday the **minister** preaches to the people in church.

mink

The **mink** is a small beast of prey.
It hunts frogs, crabs, and other little creatures in the water.

minnow

The **minnow** is a small silver-gray fish.
It never grows much longer than your finger.

minute

A **minute** is a small space of time. An hour has sixty **minutes.**

mirror

Now I must look at myself in the **mirror.**
I want to see if I am neat and tidy.

miss

When I try to bat the ball, I usually **miss** it. I fail to hit it.

mistake

A **mistake** is something done wrong.
There is a **mistake** in this picture. The knife should be on the right of the plate and the fork on the left.

Monday

Monday is the second day of the week.
On **Monday** we go back to school after the weekend.

money

When we want to buy something, we give **money** for it.
We keep **money** in a purse and we save it in a piggybank.

monkey

A **monkey** is a forest animal that can swing by its hands and feet.
Monkeys eat mostly fruit and insects.

month

The year is divided into twelve **months.**
Each **month** is about four weeks long.

moon

Tonight the **moon** looks round and big.
It is a full **moon.**

moose

The **moose** is a large animal of the deer family.
The male **moose** has huge antlers, or horns.

morning

The sun has risen. It is **morning** of a new day.

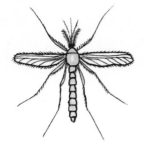

mosquito

The **mosquito** is a tiny insect that can do a lot of harm. When mosquitos bite people or animals they can cause sicknesses.

most

I have done **most** of my homework. I have finished **almost all** of it.

moth

A **moth** is a winged insect like a butterfly, but not so brightly colored. **Moths** fly mostly at night.

motorcycle

A **motorcycle** is driven by an engine. The engine makes much more noise than a car engine.

mountain

The train is running beside the **mountain.** Soon it will enter a tunnel and go through the **mountain.**

mouse

The **mouse** is a little animal with tiny ears and a long tail. The **mouse** is a rodent; it gnaws with its long front teeth like a beaver.

move
Our family is going to **move.** We are going to live in another place.

mud
I mixed earth and water together to make **mud.**
My hands and legs are all covered with **mud.**

muscle
A **muscle** moves a part of our body.
Harry has good arm **muscles.** He plays many games and helps in the garden.

museum
This is one of the **museums** in our city.
Museums have collections of things for people to see.

mushroom
Most **mushrooms** are good to eat.
Mother sometimes makes **mushroom** soup.

music
We like listening to **music.**
Father plays the piano very well.

N n

nail

This is a picture of one kind of **nail**. **Nails** are used to fasten things together.

name

My brother's **name** is Henry. That is what we call him.

napkin

On picnics we use paper **napkins** to wipe our mouth after eating. At home the dinner **napkins** are cloth.

narrow

The brook here is so **narrow** that I can jump across it. It is **not** at all **wide.**

near

We live **near** the river. It is so **close** that we can see it from our windows.

neck

Helen is wearing a silver chain around her **neck.** She is very proud of her necklace.

need
I **need** a new coat this winter. I **must have** one because my old one is too small.

needle
Mother likes to sew pretty dresses. She uses a **needle** and thread.

neighbor
Mr. Saunders lives in the house next to ours. He is our **neighbor.**

nest
A bird built its **nest** in a tree in our garden.
It will lay its eggs there and hatch out baby birds.

net
This is a **net.** Fishermen use **nets** to catch fish.

new
We have **new** schoolbooks this year. They are different from the ones we used last year.

newspaper

This is the daily **newspaper.** It has stories about all the things that happened in the last day.

next

Next week Arnold will have a birthday party. His birthday is in the week after this one.

night

The sun has set and the moon and stars are out. The **night** is beginning.

nine

Nine is a number. It is the sum of eight and one, or seven and two, or six and three, or five and four.

noise

When Paul runs down the stairs, he makes **noise.** He thumps his feet on every step.

none

None of the girls in my class have brothers. **Not any** of them do.

noon

It is **noon,** the middle of the day. The clock on our school tower shows **twelve o'clock.**

north

The wind is blowing from the **north.** That part of the world is very cold.

nose

My dog has a long cold **nose.** It is the part that he smells with.

note

Every key on the piano plays a different **note.**
Each **note** is named for a letter of the alphabet.

nothing

My lunchbox has **nothing** in it. I ate everything Mother put in it, and it is **empty.**

notice

Did you **notice** how tall Ben is getting? Did you **pay attention** to how he has grown?

November

November is the eleventh month of the year. In **November** we celebrate Thanksgiving Day.

now

We are ready to go for a walk **now.** We are ready to go **at this time.**

number

Our house is **number** 26 on Brook Street.
It is the 26th house on the street.

nurse

A **nurse** helps the doctor take care of people who are sick.

nut

A **nut** is a seed of a plant.
These three nuts are a Brazil nut, a filbert or hazelnut, and a walnut.

 **oak**

These are the leaves and the seeds of the **oak** tree.
The seeds are called acorns.

 **obey**

Uncle George has just whistled for his dog.
Bruce will **obey** and come to his master at once.

 **ocean**

Standing on the shore, we can see two steamships on the wide blue **ocean.**

October

October is the tenth month of the year.
The last day of **October** is Hallen.

 **oil**

Oil is a greasy liquid.
This bottle contains **oil** for salad dressing.
The **oil** in the can is to make machines run smoothly.

old

Here is an **old** man. He has lived many years.
His hair and beard have turned white.

olive

The **olive** is the small oily fruit of the evergreen **olive** tree.
Olives are pressed to obtain **olive** oil.

onion

The **onion** is a bulb that grows under the ground.
It is a vegetable that is eaten either raw or cooked.

open

The door is **open.**
It is warm outdoors and the **open** door lets in fresh air.

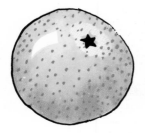

orange

The **orange** is a delicious fruit.
Orange is also a color that is named for the fruit.

ore

This railway car is loaded with **ore.**
The **ore** is stone that has metal in it.

oriole

The **oriole** is a bird that spends the summer in our country.
It builds a hanging nest that is like a little basket.

ostrich

The **ostrich** is the largest of all birds.
It cannot fly, but it runs very fast.

oven

Mother does a lot of cooking in the **oven.** She bakes cakes and roasts meat and cooks casseroles.

owl

An **owl** is a big bird with large eyes and a hooked bill.
Owls fly mostly at night. They are sometimes called **hoot owls** for the cry they make.

paddle

We like to **paddle** in the water.
We walk and jump in the shallow
part of the pool.

page

A **page** is one leaf of a book, printed
on both sides.

pail

The big **pail** is full of soapy water.
Mother is going to clean the kitchen with
it.

pain

Joan has a toothache. The **pain** is very
bad.

paint

The painters have come to **paint** our
house.
They will put a fresh layer of color
on the walls.

pair

Two of anything is a **pair.** Socks and
shoes and gloves all come in **pairs.**

palm

This tall, slim tree is a **palm.**
The leafy branches are called fronds.
Coconuts grow on some **palms.**

pan

Mother scrambles eggs in this **pan.**
She uses the same **pan** to fry many kinds
of food.

panda

The **panda** is a large animal with
black and white fur and rings
around its eyes.

pansy

A **pansy** is a garden flower that
comes in many colors.

panther

The **panther** is a large, tawny
wildcat.
The **panther** is also called
mountain lion and cougar and
puma.

paper

This towel is a **paper** towel.
Other kinds of **paper** are writing
paper and drawing **paper** and
paper napkins.

parachute

This daring man has jumped out of an airplane.
His **parachute** has opened and will bring him down safely.

parade

We watched the Thanksgiving **parade** today.
We saw giant balloons of animals, and clowns, and marching bands.

parakeet

Jan has a **parakeet** in a cage. It is a beautiful little bird of many colors.

parcel

This is the way to pack a **parcel.** It is tied carefully and has an address label pasted on it.

parents

My mother and my father are my **parents.**

park

Our **park** is like a large garden.
It has a large fountain and many tall trees.

parrot

A **parrot** is a large bird with a hooked bill.
Parrots are sometimes kept as pets. They can imitate words and laughter.

party

Betsy is having a **party.**
She is celebrating her birthday.

passengers

This train is filled with **passengers.**
The people who ride on trains, buses, boats and airplanes are called **passengers.**

paste

Paste is used to stick paper together.
I **paste** pictures in my scrapbook.

path

We took the **path** through the park. It is a **lane** for people to walk on.

patter

It is a stormy day. The rain will **patter** on the windows.

paw

The foot of an animal that has claws is called a **paw.** My dog puts out his paw to "shake hands."

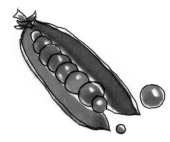

pay

Today is the last day of the month. The worker receives his **pay.**
Some people are paid in money; others receive a check to exchange for money.

pea

A **pea** is a green vegetable that grows in a pod.
Some **peas** have pods that are also good to eat.

peach

This is a ripe **peach.** A **peach** is soft and juicy, and its skin is soft as velvet.

peacock

The **peacock** is a large bird with brilliantly colored tail feathers. It struts around with the tail spread out like a fan.

peanut

The **peanut** is the seed of a vine that belongs to the pea family.
We eat **peanuts** like nuts.

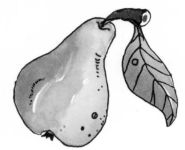

pear

The **pear** is a soft, juicy, sweet fruit. **Pears** are often stewed or canned.

pencil

I use a **pencil** for writing and drawing.
I take care not to press too hard.
If I do, the point may break off.

penguin

The **penguin** is a water bird that lives in cold countries. It cannot fly. It dives to catch fish.

penny

The **penny** is our smallest coin. It takes five **pennies** to make a nickel and ten **pennies** to make a dime.

people

There are many, many **people** in the world.
They all look different.

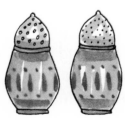

pepper

Pepper is a spice used to make foods taste better.
It is ground from peppercorns and kept in a **pepper** shaker.

perch

The **perch** is a small fish that lives in fresh water and is good to eat. The fins on its back are sharp and spiny.

perfume

I like to smell Mother's **perfume** bottles. The different scents all smell delicious.

pet

This little dog is someone's **pet.** A **pet** is a tame animal that people keep for company.

petunia

A **petunia** is a flower. This one is blue, but **petunias** grow in many colors.

pheasant

The **pheasant** is a large bird with a long tail and beautifully colored feathers. The **pheasant** lives in grassy meadows and fields of grain.

piano

I can play the **piano** quite well now. My **piano teacher** gives me a lesson each week.

pick

Our apples are ripe. Now we can **pick** them off the tree.

pickerel

The **pickerel** is a freshwater fish that is very good to eat. Another name for the **pickerel** is **pike.**

picnic

This is a cool, shady clearing in the woods.
Let us have our **picnic** here.
Mother has packed a nice lunch.

picture

I drew this **picture** myself.
Some **pictures** painted by famous artists hang in museums.

pie

Mother makes wonderful apple **pie.** She spices the apples with sugar and cinnamon and covers them with a crust.

pig

A **pig** is a farm animal. Farmers raise **pigs** for their meat.

pigeon

This **pigeon** is tame and lives in a pigeon loft.
Other **pigeons** live in parks or in wooded areas.

pike

This slim fish is a **pike.** It has sharp teeth in its large mouth.
Another name for the **pike** is **pickerel.**

pile

It was hard work to build this neat **pile** of lumber.
The separate boards are stacked up high.

pilot

A **pilot** flies an airplane or steers a boat. A **pilot** has to be very careful to keep his passengers safe.

pine

The **pine** is an evergreen tree that has its seeds in cones.
The leaves of **pine** trees are shaped like needles.

pineapple

The **pineapple** is a large fruit that grows in warm places.
Pineapples grow in Hawaii and in South America.

pink

Pink is a color. It is a pale shade of red.

pint

A **pint** is a measure of liquid. Two cups make a **pint,** and two **pints** make a quart.

pipe

A **pipe** is also a long tube to carry liquids. Water comes into the house through **pipes.**

pipe

This is Grandfather's **pipe.** He puts tobacco in it and smokes it.

pit

We have dug ourselves a **pit.** It is like a real den covered over with branches.

plain

This dress is very **plain.** It does not have much trimming to make it look pretty.

plant

In this picture you can see all the parts of a **plant.**
It has roots and stems and leaves and flowers.

please

"**Please,**" says Fritz as he sits up and begs.
We say **please** when we ask for something.

pleat

A **pleat** is a fold made in cloth.
The skirt of this dress is **pleated.**

pliers

A pair of **pliers** is a tool for holding or bending things. Some **pliers** can also cut wire.

plow

A **plow** cuts and turns over the soil before seeds are planted.
On the farm the **plow** is pulled by a tractor.

plum

A **plum** is a juicy fruit with a shiny purple skin. **Plums** are dried to make prunes.

pocket

I have **pockets** in my overalls. I carry small things in my **pockets.**

point

When Nancy sees an airplane, she will **point** with her finger to show her brother where it is in the sky.

poison

POISON is dangerous. **Poison** can make people very sick if they eat or drink it.

poison ivy

Poison ivy is a plant that grows in fields and hedges.
When you touch it, the oil in the plant causes little blisters or sores on your skin.

polar bear

The **polar bear** is a large animal with white fur.
The **polar bear** lives in the cold North. It doesn't mind the ice and snow.

police

The **police** help to keep our city safe.
They are the ones to ask if we need help.
This policeman is taking the little boy across the street.

polish

The carpenter has made a table.
Now he can **polish** it to make it shine.

pond

A **pond** is a body of water. It is smaller than a lake.

pony

A **pony** is a kind of horse that is very small. **Ponies** are fun for children to ride.

poodle

A **poodle** is a dog with thick, curly fur. Its fur is often cut in a fancy trim.

pool

We have a small **pool** in our backyard. The water is not deep, and we wade in it. The big children go to the city **pool** to swim and dive off the deep end.

poppy

The **poppy** is a plant with large flowers.
Some **poppies** are red. Others are white or purple.

porch

A **porch** is a covered deck attached to a house.
Some **porches** are closed in with glass to keep them warm.

porcupine

A **porcupine** is a rodent, or gnawing animal. Its body is covered with sharp quills.

port

Ships dock at a **port.** They load and unload goods at this place that is safe from storms.

poster

This brightly colored **poster** tells us that the circus is coming to town.
We make **posters** in school to let people know about our spring fair.

potato

A **potato** is a vegetable that grows underground.
Potatoes are good to eat peeled and mashed or baked in their skins.

pound

A **pound** is a measure of weight. I bought a **pound** of butter, and the grocer weighed it on his scale.

prairie

The **prairie** is land with rich soil that is good for growing grain. In this picture a tractor pulls a machine to cut the ripe wheat.

pray

It is time for Jane to **pray.** She is saying her evening **prayer** before she goes to bed.

prefer

I **prefer** chocolate to vanilla ice cream.
I **like** chocolate **better than** vanilla.

present

Mary has a birthday **present** for Henry. She gives him a gaily wrapped **gift.**

preserve

Our cherry tree had lots of cherries this year.
Mother is going to **preserve** them so we can eat them in the winter.

press

I have found a four-leaf clover, and I am going to **press** it.
I will put it between the pages of a book to keep it for good luck.

pretend

We like to dress up in grownup clothes and **pretend** to be other people.

pretty

A **pretty** thing is something that is nice to look at.
I painted a **pretty** pattern on this egg. Now I shall decorate the other one.

price

"What is the **price** of grapes today?" asks the woman. "Ninety-eight cents a pound," answers the storekeeper.

prick

Mary must be careful not to **prick** her finger on the thorns of the rosebush.

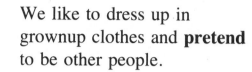

print

I can **print** letters. The two letters I have printed here stand for my name, Henry Osgood.

propeller

A **propeller** helps an airplane to fly.
It spins very fast and pulls the plane through the air.

prune

A **prune** is a dried fruit made from a plum.
Prunes are good to eat cooked with spices.

puddle

It has been raining hard today. I splash in a **puddle.**

pull

The dog does not like being tied up. See him **pull** at his chain.

pump

There is not enough air in my bicycle tire. I shall **pump** more air into it.

pumpkin

A **pumpkin** is a very large orange-colored fruit. Mother makes **pumpkin** pie.

pupil

I am a **pupil** in school. I am one of the children who are taught in my school.

purple

Purple is a color made by mixing red and blue.

push

This motorcycle has had a breakdown. The rider has to **push** it.

put

It is very cold. Mother said, "**Put** on your heavy coat."
I **put** my hands in my pockets to keep them warm.

pyramid

This huge stone structure is a **pyramid.** **Pyramids** like this were built thousands of years ago in Egypt.

Q q

quarrel

When children play too hard, they sometimes **quarrel**. They **argue** and call each other names.

quart

A **quart** is a measure of liquid. Two pints make a **quart,** and two **quarts** make a half gallon.

quarter

A **quarter** is a coin. It is worth twenty-five pennies or five nickels.

queen

This is the **queen** in the story of "Snow White and the Seven Dwarfs." She is wearing a crown on her head.

question

If you ask your teacher a **question,** she will give you the answer. She will tell you what you want to know.

quiet

An Indian is very **quiet** as he creeps through the forest. He **makes no noise.**

R r

rabbit

The wild **rabbit** looks like a small hare.
Rabbit families live together in holes in the ground called warrens.

raccoon

The **raccoon** is a small animal that hunts at night and always washes its food.
The **raccoon** has a face like a mask and a bushy tail with white rings.

race

These boys are running a **race**.
They are trying to see who can run the fastest.

radiator

The **radiator** is a metal container that holds steam or hot water to keep a room warm.

radio

This small **radio** receives sound through the air.
We can listen to music or the latest news on the **radio**.

radish

The **radish** is a vegetable.
We eat the red root which is spicy and crisp.

raft

Four huge logs have been fastened together to make a **raft.**
Workmen are floating the logs down the river to the mill.

rain

A heavy, dark cloud is moving across the sky. It has started to **rain.**

rake

Jack means to use this **rake** to help gather the dead leaves on the lawn.

raspberry

This is a red **raspberry.**
It is a small juicy fruit that we like raw, or made into jam.
Some **raspberries** are black.

rat

The **rat** is a rodent. It has teeth for gnawing.
Rats destroy grain and other foods. They sometimes carry diseases.

rather

Sally would **rather** read than play cards. She **prefers** to read a book.

raven

The **raven** is a large bird that is in the crow family.
It has a sharp beak and shiny black feathers.

read

I like to **read** books. Best of all, I like **reading** stories about animals.

recess

The children play games in the schoolyard at **recess.**
When **recess** is over, they go back to class.

red pepper

This is a hot **red pepper.**
It is made into a sharp spice called cayenne pepper.

reed

A **reed** is a kind of grass that grows in wet places.
These **reeds** are sometimes called cattails.

reindeer

The **reindeer** is a large animal that lives in the far North.
The Eskimos use **reindeer** like our cows or horses.

reins

The driver pulls on the **reins** to tell the horses to stop.

repeat

The teacher says a new word, and the children **repeat** it. They **say it again** to help them remember it.

reply

Mary received a letter from her friend. She will **reply** to it. She will **answer** the letter.

rescue

This boy waded into deep water. The man jumped after him to **rescue** him.

rest

"Let us **rest** for five minutes," said Arthur. "Let us sit quietly or take a nap in the shade."

return

The songbirds fly south when the weather becomes cold, but they will **return.** They will **come back** in the spring.

The **rhinoceros** is a huge water animal that lives in Africa and Asia.
It has a thick hide and a horn on its nose.

rhyme

Words **rhyme** when they **sound alike.** June, moon, soon, tune are words that **rhyme.**

ribbon

A **ribbon** is a narrow strip of silk or satin. We use **ribbon** to tie gaily wrapped packages.

rice

Rice is a grain that grows in water fields. We eat **rice** as a part of a meal or made into **rice** pudding.

riddle

Peter asked Tom a **riddle.**
Tom could not work out the answer
to the **puzzling question.**

ride

When we **ride,** we are carried by an
animal or a machine.
Carol **rides** her pony and Charles **rides**
his bicycle.

right

Cars, trucks, and bicycles in America
must stay on the **right** side of the
road. That is a rule of traffic.

ring

The children are dancing in a **ring.**
They are holding hands in a **circle.**
Mother has a beautiful wedding **ring.**
It is a **circle** of gold that she wears on
her finger.

ripe

These plums are **ripe.** They are dark
blue and soft and **ready to eat.**

rise   We **rise** soon after the sun **rises.** We get out of bed after the sun has come up.

river   This broad **river** flows th fields and valleys. It finally flows into the sea.

road   A **road** is a way for going from one place to another.
In the city the **roads** are called **streets.**
In the country they are called **highways** or **freeways.**

roast   This is a **roast** of meat sizzling in the pan. It has been cooked in the oven.

robin   The **robin** is a large bird with a black head and tail and a reddish breast.

rocks   The **rocks** on this coast are very dangerous.
Some of the **rocks** are underwater.
Ships have to sail carefully.

roll

I can **roll** the barrel because it is round. A bicycle **rolls** because its wheels are round.

rolls

Mother baked these **rolls** for dinner. A **roll** is a little loaf of bread for one person.

roof

Our house has a sloping **roof.** That helps the rain to run off.

room

I have just been given a **room** of my own.
It contains my bed and my bookcase and my clothes closet.

rooster

This is the **rooster** of our chicken house.
He is very brightly colored. He crows loudly every day at sunrise.

roots

The **roots** of this plant grow in the earth.
Plants draw water and food from the earth th their **roots.**

rope

Rope is heavy cord. We use **rope** to tie large packages.
A jump **rope** is a children's toy.

rose

The **rose** is one of the most beautiful of flowers.
Roses grow in many colors and shapes and sizes. They all have a sweet perfume.

row

We are all standing side by side in a **row** to have our picture taken.

row

We are going for a boat ride on the lake.
Philip will **row** the boat with the oars.

rub

Bill does not like his drawing. He is going to **rub** it out with an eraser.

rubber

The **rubber** tree grows in hot, damp countries.
When its bark is cut, thick sap drips out.

rug

I like to lie on the **rug** in front of the fireplace.
The **rug** is a soft **covering** for the floor.

ruler

When I want to draw a straight line, I use a **ruler.**
The **ruler** can also tell me the size of my piece of paper.

run

Paul is late for school today. He must **run** to get there.
He must **go very fast.**

rust

These iron railings are turning reddish-brown at the top. They are beginning to **rust.**

S s

sack

Robert is carrying a heavy **sack.**
The weight of the **sack** makes him stoop.

sad

Jimmy is feeling very **sad** today. He is **unhappy** because he has lost his favorite top.

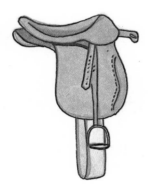

saddle

This **saddle** is for the horse's back.
It makes a place for the rider to sit safely.

sails

The boat moves over the water because the wind blows into its white **sails.**

St. Bernard

The **St. Bernard** is a big, furry dog. He is so gentle and friendly that small children can ride on his back.

salad

We eat **salad** with dinner almost every night.
I like tossed **salad** with all kinds of greens.

salmon

The **salmon** is a large fish that lives both in rivers and in the sea.
Its pink flesh is very good to eat.

salt

Mother keeps the **salt** for cooking in this big box.
A little **salt** makes food taste better.

sand

Sand is rock that has been ground into tiny pieces.
We like to dig in **sand** piles or at the beach.

sandals

Sandals are fun to wear in the summer.
I can wear them without socks.

sandwich

I can make my own **sandwich** for lunch. I put peanut butter and jelly between two pieces of bread.

Santa Claus

Here comes **Santa Claus** carrying his bag of gifts for Christmas.

sap

Sap is the juice of plants that carries food from the earth. The **sap** flows to the tip of every leaf.

sapling

The gardener is planting a **sapling.** It will grow into a large tree.

Saturday

Saturday is the last day of the week and the first day of the weekend.

saw

A branch of the tree is growing too close to the window.
Albert is cutting it off with a **saw.**

scales

With these **scales** I can weigh things.
I put a pound weight on one side and add things to the other side until the two sides balance.

scales

A fish has many tiny plates on its skin to protect it from being hurt. The plates are called **scales.**

scar

In the palm of my left hand there is a **scar.**
It is the place where a cut has healed.

scare

Jim dressed up in a sheet to try to **scare** us. But he couldn't **frighten** us that way.

scarf

This is my favorite **scarf.** It is made of wool and is soft and warm around my neck.

scent

Mother's perfume has a lovely **scent.**
It has a very sweet **odor.**

school

This is our new **school.** All the classrooms are on one floor so that we can get around easily.

scissors

These four kinds of **scissors** are made for cutting different things.

Scottish terrier

This little dog with his big head and wiry coat is a **Scottish terrier.** Most people call him a Scottie.

scout

Paul is dressed up like an Indian **scout.**
He is pretending to watch out for danger to his tribe.

scrape

Today we are having carrots with dinner.
I am helping Mother to **scrape** them. I **rub off** the outer skin.

screw

A **screw** is used to fasten pieces of wood together.
Daddy uses a screwdriver for **screws** like these.

scrub

I am going to **scrub** the kitchen floor. I will use soapy water with this strong brush.

sea horse

The **sea horse** is a strange little fish with a long tail and a head that looks like a horse's head.
The **sea horse** swims upright like this in the water.

seal

The **seal** is an animal that lives in the ocean.
Seals have fins and tails like fish, instead of legs.

seam

The **seam** in Elizabeth's jacket has split open.
The two pieces of cloth that were sewn together have come apart.

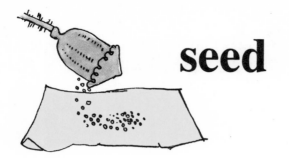

seed

When you open the **seed** case of a poppy, all the **seeds** roll out.
All plants, even trees, grow from **seeds.**

seesaw

A **seesaw** is a board balanced over a center piece. When the child on one end goes up, the child on the other end goes down.

sentence

A **sentence** is written on this piece of paper.
A **sentence** is a group of words that give a message.

September

September is the ninth month of the year. It is the month when school begins.

set

Evelyn is going to **set** the table.
She begins with the plates. Then she will bring the silver and the napkins.

seven

Seven is a number. It is the sum of six and one, or five and two, or four and three.

shade

Let's play on the lawn. The leaves of the elm tree will **shade** us from the sun.

shadow

My **shadow** goes everywhere with me. It is the shaded place made by my body between the sun and the ground.

shake

The plums are ripe. If I **shake** the tree, the plums will fall to the ground.

shape

This jug has a beautiful **shape.** It is smooth and simple.

shark

The **shark** is a huge fish that lives in the ocean. It is a fierce hunter.

sharp

This knife is very **sharp.** It cuts very well.

sheep

In the spring the farmer shears the **sheep.**
The **sheep** on the right has already had its wool shorn to make cloth.

sheet

I can make my bed by myself. This is the bottom **sheet.**
I will put another **sheet** on top of it and then cover the bed with a blanket.

shelf

Mother has an open **shelf** near the stove for the cooking things she uses often.

shell

My cousin Douglas collects beautiful **shells** like this one that he found on the beach.
A **shell** was once the home of a small sea animal.

shelter

We have taken **shelter** under this tree.
Its leaves will protect us from the rain.

ship

A **ship** is a large boat that can travel long distances.
This **ship** is a freighter that carries cargo.
A small sailboat is coming toward it.

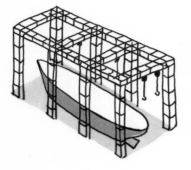

shipyard

Ships are built in a **shipyard.**
When they are finished, the ships slide down tracks into the water.

shirt

Mother bought me a new **shirt.** It is made of fine, soft cotton.

shoe

The shoemaker has repaired my **shoes.**
He nailed a new leather sole on the bottom of each **shoe.**

shoot

We are going to **shoot** at a target with a slingshot.
The one whose pebble hits the center is the best shot.

shop

We **shop** for the weekend on Fridays. I help Mother with the grocery **shopping.**

shore

The **shore** of the ocean or the lake is sandy. The land there has been ground into fine grains.

shoulder

Allan is carrying a suitcase on his **shoulder.** He is a strong boy.

shout

Kenneth likes to **shout.** He likes to make a lot of noise when he speaks.

shovel

When we have a snowstorm, I like to help Daddy **shovel** the walk clear of snow.

shower

The weather is very hot. This is our third **shower** today.

shrimp

This is a **shrimp.** It is a small sea animal.
Shrimp are good to eat in salad or in a baked dish.

sick

Jill is feeling **sick** today. She has a cold.
Sick is another word for **ill.**

sieve

Mother uses this **sieve** when she is cooking.
She strains foods like rice in it to get out the water.

signal

The railroad **signal** is going up. It tells the engineer that the train may go through.

silent

We must be **silent** when we are in the library. We must not talk or make noise.

silk

Alice is wearing a **silk** dress. It is very soft and smooth.
Silk thread is made by silkworms for their cocoons.

silo

This tower with the round top is a **silo.**
The farmer uses the **silo** to store feed for
his animals.

silver

This spoon is made of **silver.**
Silver is a valuable metal that is also
used for making fine jewelry.

sinew

The **sinew** joins the muscles to the
bones. It helps the muscles move the
bones at the joints.

sing

Lucy has a good voice. She can **sing**
well. She can make music with her
voice.

sister

My **sister** is the daughter of my
mother and father.

sit

I got up from my chair. Now the old lady can **sit** in my place.

six

Six is a number. It is the sum of five and one, or four and two, or three and three.

size

The **size** is the measure of a thing. Shoes and clothes are marked with their **size** to tell us if they will fit us.

skates

Skates help us to move fast on our feet. **Roller skates** have four wheels for each foot. **Ice skates** have a sharp blade that glides over the ice.

skeleton

This is the **skeleton** of a cat. It is the bones of the animal. You can see dinosaur **skeletons** in the museum.

skip

It is good exercise to **skip** rope. We swing the rope round and round and jump lightly over it.

skirt

Dorothy has a new yellow **skirt.** She wears it hanging from her waist, below her brown blouse.

skunk

The **skunk** is a small animal with a white stripe and a bushy tail. It protects itself by spraying enemies with a bad-smelling fluid.

sky

The **sky** is beautiful today. The **sky** is blue and dotted with large and small clouds.

skyscraper

A **skyscraper** is a huge office building. It may have as many as one hundred floors.

sled

We are going out to play with my **sled** in the new snow.
We will slide down the hill and climb back up to slide down again.

sleep

At night we go to **sleep.**
We close our eyes and rest until the morning comes.
Small children need more **sleep.**
They take a **nap** in the afternoon.

sleet

When the air is cold and rain freezes as it falls, the rain is called **sleet.**

sleigh

A sleigh is a large sled that is pulled by a horse.
Santa Claus's **sleigh** is pulled by reindeer.

slide

We have a **slide** in our park.
It is fun to climb the ladder and **slide** to the bottom.

slippers

These **slippers** are soft and warm.
I put them on when I come in from the cold.

slow

Donald is pushing the wheelbarrow up the hill. It is **slow** work because the load is heavy.

small

Katy is a very **small** girl. She is **not large.**

smell

Jane likes to **smell** the roses. They have a lovely scent.

smile

When I am happy, I **smile.** The corners of my mouth turn up, and my eyes are bright.

smoke

Our neighbors have a coal furnace in their house.
Now and then, thick, black **smoke** comes out of the chimney.

snail

A **snail** carries its house on its back.
It never leaves its shell behind.

snake

A **snake** has no feet. It glides along
the ground or up a tree.
Some **snakes** poison their enemies
when they bite.

snow

The **snow** is falling heavily.
Snowflakes look lovely as they float
down from the sky.

snow-capped

This **snow-capped** mountain is called
Fujiyama. It is in Japan. The top of
Fujiyama has snow on it all year round.

snow plow

The **snow plow** starts
work when the snow
has stopped falling.
It must clear the streets
for cars and trucks.

soap

This is a new piece of **soap.**
It has a pleasant smell. It makes puffy
white lather when I wash with it.

soar

Have you ever seen an eagle **soar**
through the sky? It glides through the
air almost without moving its wings.

socks

These are my favorite **socks.**
They keep my feet feeling
comfortable inside my shoes.

sofa

We have a new **sofa** in our living room.
It is a wide seat with soft cushions and a
high back.

soil

The **soil** in our flower beds is very rich. It
grows many kinds of flowers.

sole

A **sole** is a flat fish that lives in the
ocean. **Sole** are caught for food all
around the world.

solid　My building blocks are **solid.** They are **not hollow.** Each block is wood all the way through.

son　Jack is his parents' **son.** He is their boy child.

sorry　I have stepped on Vera's foot. "I am **sorry,** Vera. I did not mean to do it."

soup　**Soup** is a food made by boiling meat and vegetables in water. My favorite **soups** are chicken soup and pea soup.

sour　This apple is **sour.** It makes my mouth pucker. It is not ripe enough to eat.

south　**South** is the direction to your right as you face the early morning sun. **South** is at the bottom of a map.

sow

I want to **sow** some seeds in this earth. I spread them evenly so the flowers will not be crowded.

spade

This is my **spade.** It has a flat blade so that I can dig a straight ditch.

spaniel

This little dog with long ears and a silky coat is a **spaniel.** It is a **cocker spaniel.**

spark

A **spark** is a small bit of fire. **Sparks** are flying from the funnel of this engine from the coal burning in the furnace.

sparrow

The **sparrow** is one bird that stays with us all winter long. It chirps gaily, but it cannot sing.

spawn

Spawn is the eggs of fish or frogs.
They are laid in the bottom of the water.
Soon they hatch into baby fish or frogs.

speak

When we **speak,** we make word sounds with our voice.

spell

I have learned to **spell** many words. I can name the letters that make up the words.

spice

The dried leaves of these plants are **spices.**
Mother uses **spice** to flavor food.

spider

A **spider** is an eight-legged insect that catches other insects for its food.
The **spider** spins a web like this one to trap flies.

spill

If I tip the milk bottle too far, the milk will **spill**.
It will **run out**.

spinach

Spinach is a leafy green vegetable. Mother boils **spinach** or serves it raw in salad.

spokes

Two of these wheels have **spokes**.
The wagon wheel has thick **spokes**.
The bicycle wheel has thin **spokes**.
The car wheel has no **spokes**.

sponge

This round, yellow **sponge** is a dead sea animal.
The small, red **sponge** is made of rubber.
We use them both for cleaning.

spool

Mother's sewing box has many colors of thread. Each color is wound on a **spool**.

spoon

We eat soup or soft things like pudding and ice cream with a **spoon.** A **spoon** is like a tiny cup that holds food.

spread

Alice is hungry. She can **spread** butter on a slice of bread.

spring

The snow has melted and **spring** has come to the valley.
The trees are in bud and the flowers are beginning to bloom.

spring

Water is coming out of the ground here. It is a **spring.**
Some **springs** turn into brooks and then into rivers.

spruce

This tree is a **spruce.**
It is an evergreen tree of the pine family.
Its needles are pointed and sharp.

square

This is a **square.** It has four sides of the same length and four corners.

squash

Squash is a vegetable that grows in different shapes and colors. Some kinds of **squash** are **yellow squash** and **green squash** and **butternut squash.**

squeak

This door **squeaks.**
The metal hinges make a noise as they rub together.
Robert has an oilcan to oil the hinges.

squirrel

The **squirrel** with its big, bushy tail is a rodent.
It gnaws its food with long sharp front teeth.

stadium

This is our school **stadium.**
People come to it to see students play all kinds of sports.
We have baseball and basketball and football teams.

stain

Audrey has been careless.
She has made a **stain** on her new dress.

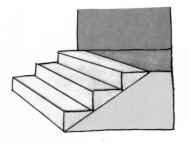

stairs

These are some **stairs** in our house.
We walk up them to get to the floor above.

stake

A **stake** is a long, thin piece of wood.
This **stake** is helping to make a young tree grow straight.

stamp

Daddy has brought me a new **stamp** for my **stamp** collection.
He receives letters from far places with interesting **stamps** on them.

star

What is the name of that bright **star** near the moon?
That is the evening **star**.
It is the first one we see when night falls.

starfish

The **starfish** is a sea animal. Its five arms give it the shape of a star. That is how it got its name.

starling

This **starling** is perched on our bird nesting box. **Starlings** bother other birds and drive them away from their nests.

station

A **station** is a stopping place for a train or a bus. It is also called a depot.

steam

The water in the pot is boiling. It is changing into **steam.** The **steam** is strong enough to push the lid off the pot.

steel

This is a **steel beam.** **Steel** is a hard, strong metal that is used to make many useful things like machines and pipes.

steep

The hill behind our house is very **steep.** It is almost straight up and down.

steer

When I ride my bicycle, I have to **steer** carefully.
I have to **guide** the bike straight down the walk.

step

When I go out with Daddy, I try to walk as he does.
I like to keep in **step** with him.

stew

Mother makes delicious **stew.**
She cuts up beef or lamb with vegetables and boils them all together.

stiff

It is very cold today. If I take my hand out of my pocket, it soon gets **stiff** with cold so that I can't move it easily.

sting

A bee **sting** hurts because the bee puts a tiny bit of poison in the skin where it pricks.

stir

Ronald has a cup of milk. He is going to **stir** in syrup to make chocolate milk.

stomach

Everything we eat goes into our **stomach.**
Food goes down the throat to the **stomach** to be digested.

stone

These three things were made of **stone** by men who did not know what iron was.
They are the tip of a lance, an arrowhead, and an ax.

store

We have a fine grocery **store** on our street.
Other **stores** sell meat, or candy, or clothing.

stork

The **stork** is a large bird with long legs and a large bill.
Storks catch fish by wading in deep water.

storm

A **storm** is coming.
See how the wind blows the trees.
Soon we will have heavy rain.

story

Grandmother is going to tell me a **story**.
I like the **story** of Peter Rabbit and the fairy **tale** of Snow White.

stove

Mother cooks on a **stove** like this. It is a gas **stove**.
Some **stoves** are heated with electricity instead of gas.

strap

This is a strong leather **strap**.
I use it to fasten my books together when I carry them to school.

straw

After the grain has been threshed, what is left is **straw**.
The farmer uses the **straw** to make warm beds for his animals.

strawberry

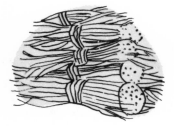

The **strawberry** is a bright red fruit that grows on a vine.
I like **strawberries** and cream and **strawberry shortcake**.

streetcar

The **streetcar** carries people
from place to place.
Most cities today use buses
instead of **streetcars.**

strong

The boys on our tug-of-war team
are **strong.**
They have good muscles and can
pull harder than the other team.

study

We **study** hard to learn our lessons.
We read our book and think about
what it tells us.

sturgeon

The **sturgeon** is a very large
fish.
It has tough skin with rows
of bony scales.

submarine

A **submarine** is a ship
that can sail on top of
or under the water.
Some of the ships in
the navy are
submarines.

subway

In many big cities the people
travel by **subway.**
The **subway** is a railroad that
runs under the ground.

sugarcane

Sugarcane is a tall grass that grows in hot countries.
Sugar is made from the sap of the **sugarcane.**

summer

Summer is the hot time of the year.
In the **summer** we have no school.
Father takes a vacation from work.

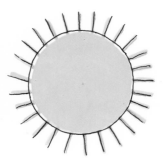

sun

The **sun** is the nearest star to earth.
The **sun** keeps us warm and makes things grow.

Sunday

Sunday is the first day of the week. It is a day of rest for most people.

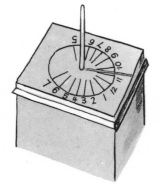

sundial

A **sundial** is a very old way to tell time.
The sun makes a shadow on the marker on a dial, pointing to the time.

sunflower

The **sunflower** is a tall flower with very large blossoms that look like huge daisies.
People like to eat **sunflower** seeds.

supper

Supper is the last meal of the day. We should eat light foods for **supper.**

swallow

The **swallow** is a small bird with long, narrow wings and a forked tail.
In cold weather, **swallows** fly to warmer places.
When spring comes, they return.

swamp

A **swamp** is a watery, muddy place.
Reeds and water lilies grow in the water of a **swamp.**

swan

The **swan** is a large, white water bird.
Its long neck is good for dipping into the water to collect food.

sweater

My new **sweater** is made of brightly colored wool yarn. It was knitted with two knitting needles.

swim

This is the pool where I am going to learn to **swim.** I will learn to move my arms and legs to keep afloat.

swing

Daddy has hung a **swing** for me on a branch of the apple tree. I know how to move my body so that I can **swing** up high.

swordfish

The **swordfish** is a large ocean fish. The sword is a long bone with which the fish spears its food.

syllable

The name E-LIZ-A-BETH has four **syllables.** In the picture each **syllable** has a different color. Knowing syllables helps us pronounce words.

T t

table

This is our dining room **table.**
We use it for our meals.
In the living room we have a **card table** for playing games.

tadpole

A **tadpole** is a baby frog or a baby toad.
After a while the **tadpole** grows legs and its tail drops off.
Then it is a frog or toad.

tag

Tag is a game we play in the schoolyard.
The person who is "it" has to try to catch and **tag** the other players.

tail

Most animals have a **tail** at the end of their body. Cats and monkeys have long **tails.** Rabbits have almost no **tail** at all.

tailor

The **tailor** is a person who makes clothes just for one person.
He measures the person and sews the cloth to fit perfectly.

tale

A **tale** is a story. Fairy **tales** are made-up stories about giants and witches.

talk

Baby Dick is learning to **talk.**
He can already say Dada, Mama, and
No.

tall

Henry is going to measure himself with
the tape measure. He wants to find out
how **tall** he is.

tame

The animals at the children's zoo are
tame. None of them will hurt us.

tan

Tan is a color. It is a light yellowish
brown.
When we go to the beach, our skin
becomes **tan** from the sun.

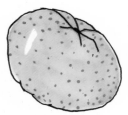

tangerine

A **tangerine** is very much
like a small orange.
It has many seeds. Its skin
peels off easily.

tanker

A **tanker** is a ship made to carry
oil and other liquids.

tar
The big steam roller has rolled the new road smooth.
The workman is spraying **tar** on the gravel.

taste
Cake has a sweet **taste.** "This cake **tastes** delicious," says Timothy.

tea
This is a branch of a **tea plant.**
Tea is made from its dried leaves.

teacher
This is our **teacher.**
She helps us to learn our lessons in school.

tear
Norma is crying. A **tear** runs down her cheek.

tear

How did Robert **tear** his jacket?
The sleeve has a large **rip** in it.

telephone

The **telephone** is ringing.
Jane answers the phone to
find out who is calling.

telescope

My big brother has a
telescope.
It has a glass eyepiece that
makes the stars look much
closer.

ten

Ten is a number. It is the sum of nine and
one, or eight and two, or seven and three,
or six and four, or five and five.

tennis

Lawn **tennis** is the name of this
game.
It is played with a racket and a
rubber ball covered with felt.

tent

We have put up our **tent** in the backyard.
Mother may let us sleep in it tonight.

terry cloth

Bath towels are made of **terry cloth.** It is a thick cotton cloth with lots of tiny loops that soak up water quickly.

test

Every week our teacher gives us a **test.** We must write down the answers to questions she asks us.

thank

When someone does me a favor, I **thank** him to let him know I am grateful.

thaw

The cold weather is ending.
The snow is beginning to **thaw.**
Our snowman is going to **melt.**

theater

This building is a **theater.**
People go to the **theater** to see a play or a movie.

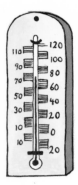

thermometer

This **thermometer** measures the temperature of the air.
The figures on it tell whether it is warm or cold.

thief

What is the **thief** doing in the night?
He is trying to steal something from this house.

thirsty

Marjorie is **thirsty.**
She is going to drink a glass of water.

thorn

A **thorn** is a sharp-pointed part of a branch or stem. Roses have many **thorns.**

thread

Mother is trying to **thread** a needle.
She will use the **thread** to sew a button onto my shirt.

three

Three is a number. It is the sum of two and one.

throat

The **throat** is the inside of the neck. If your **throat** is sore, it may make you cough.

throw

This is not a good place to **throw** a basketball.
We might break a window.

thumb

Tim is touching his **thumb.**
The **thumb** makes it possible for us to pick up things with our fingers.

thunder

Thunder is the sound made by lightning.
Lightning can be dangerous, but **thunder** is only a noise.

Thursday

Thursday is the fifth day of the week. It comes between Wednesday and Friday.

ticket

A **ticket** allows us to ride on a bus or train.
We pay money for a **ticket.**

tickle

Dan is trying to **tickle** his sister with a grass stalk.
He hopes to make her laugh.

tidy

Jean keeps her room very **tidy.** She makes her bed in the morning and hangs up her clothes. She puts all her toys away in the toy chest.

tie

Marion's shoelace is loose. She must **tie** it again.

tie

This is a **tie** that I wear with my best suit. It goes around my neck under the collar of my shirt.

tiger

The **tiger** is a large wildcat with black stripes on tawny fur.
The **tiger** is very beautiful but also very dangerous.

tiny

The mosquito is a **tiny** insect. It is **very small,** but it has a very big bite.

tire

Our car has a flat **tire.** The rubber covering of one wheel has a hole in it. It won't hold air anymore.

tired

Viola is **tired.** She has played too hard and needs to rest.

title

A **title** is the **name** of a book or a poem or a song.

toad

The **toad** is a jumping animal like a frog.
The **toad** lives on land but lays its eggs in water.

toadstool

The **toadstool** looks like a bright-colored mushroom. Never touch a **toadstool.** It can be poisonous.

toast

We usually have **toast** for breakfast. Mother heats slices of bread until they are brown.

tobacco

The **tobacco** plant grows in warm parts of our country. Cigarettes and cigars are made out of dried **tobacco.**

tomato

This is a juicy, ripe **tomato.** We use the **tomato** as a vegetable, but it is really a fruit.

tongue

The **tongue** is a part of the mouth. We taste with our **tongue.** It also helps us to talk.

tools

These are some of Daddy's **tools.**
They are a hammer, two wrenches, a file, and a gimlet.

tooth

There was a tiny hole in my front **tooth.**
Donald is looking to see how the dentist has fixed it.

top

Shirley's book is on the **top** shelf.
She cannot reach it.

top

I shall play with my **top** today.
I have a long piece of string to make it spin for a long time.

touch

Never **touch** the stove when Mother is cooking. If you put your hand on it you will be burned.

towel

Towels are used to dry things.
Mother uses a dish **towel.**
I have a bath **towel** so big it covers
me up.

tower

In some old towns a **tower** like this
still stands.
Towers once were part of the town
wall.

town

This is the middle of a small **town.**
It is where the stores and offices are
built.

toy

Sometimes Irene likes to play with her
little brother's **toy.**
This **toy** is a bear with legs that move.

trace

It is fun to **trace** pictures from a
book.
I put thin paper over a picture and
trace it with a pencil.

tracks

These are railroad **tracks.**
The wheels of the train roll on the
tracks.

tractor

The farmer's **tractor** has a
strong engine.
It can pull heavy farm machines.

traffic

The **traffic** in the streets is
dangerous.
The cars and trucks move in all
directions.

trail

When we go to the woods, we follow a
trail. It is a **path** made by many people
going the same way.

train

The railroad crossing is closed to
make the cars stop.
The **train** is about to pass through.

trap

There is a mouse in our basement.
The mouse is near the **trap.**

trash

Jill and I clean up the kitchen. Jill
washes the dishes. I take out the
trash.

tray

This **tray** is made of wood.
It has handles to make it easy to carry.

tree

This **tree** is old. It has a thick trunk and
many branches.

triangle

This figure has three corners.
It is a **triangle.**

trickle

The water faucet is broken.
A **trickle** of water is running
down the wall.

tricycle

Cynthia is riding a **tricycle.**
She can balance on three
wheels.

trip

On our last vacation, we made a **trip** to
the mountains.
We traveled from our home on a train.

trousers

My brother is wearing his
first **trousers.** They are the
long pants that are part of a
suit.

trout

The **trout** is a fish that lives in rivers
and lakes.
It is very good to eat.

truck

This is a **dairy truck.**
The **truck** driver travels around
collecting cans of milk from dairy
farmers.

trumpet   A **trumpet** is a musical instrument made of brass.

trunk   The **trunk** is the main stem of the tree.
The roots hold the **trunk** firmly in the earth.

trust   Mother knows she can **trust** me. She can believe that I will behave as I should.

truth   Children should always tell the **truth**. They should never lie.

try   I am going to **try** to cook.
I will see if I can fry an egg.

Tuesday   **Tuesday** is the third day of the week. It comes between Monday and Wednesday.

tug   The small steamer is strong enough to tow the huge freighter into the harbor.
The small boat is a **tug.**

tulip

The **tulip** is a flower that grows from a bulb.
Tulips bloom in the spring in many beautiful colors.

tuna

The **tuna** is a large ocean fish.
Tuna is very good to eat.

tune

A **tune** is the music of a song. We learn the **tune** so that we can sing our favorite song.

turkey

The **turkey** is a large bird.
Most Americans have **turkey** for Thanksgiving dinner.

turtle

This is my pet **turtle.**
It can pull its head, legs, and tail into its hard, bony shell.

twin

Sally is my **twin** sister. She was born on the same day as I was.

two

Two is a number. It is the sum of one and one.

U u

ugly

Rover has been rolling in the mud.
His fur is sticky and dirty.
He looks **ugly.**

umbrella

Mary and Jo are holding
their mother's **umbrella** to
keep off the rain.

uncle

My **Uncle** John is Mother's brother.
I have another **uncle** who is Daddy's
brother.

underwear

Underwear is the
clothing that we wear
under our dress or our
suit.

undress

When it is time for bed, we
undress and put on our
pajamas.
We **take off** our daytime
clothes.

uneven

The sidewalk outside our school
is very **uneven.** It is **rough.**

unhappy

Larry is **unhappy** because it is raining.
He is **sad** because he will not be able to play outdoors.

uniform

All policemen are dressed in the same way.
They wear a **uniform.**

United States of America

The **United States** is our country.
It is called U.S.A. for short.

universe

The **universe** is made up of the sun, the moon, and all the planets and stars.

upstairs

The bedrooms in our house are **upstairs.** They are on the second floor. We climb the stairs to get **upstairs.**

V v

vacant

Before we moved into our house, it had been **vacant** for a long time. No one had lived in it.

vacation

Children have **vacation** from school for the whole summer.
Daddies usually have **time off** from work for only a few weeks.

vaccinate

The doctor at school will **vaccinate** the children.
He will protect them from getting diseases.

valentine

One of my best friends sent me this **valentine.**
It tells me that I have a very good friend.

valley

A **valley** lies between two mountains.
Often a river flows at the bottom of the **valley.**

242

van

The moving company brought our furniture to our new home in a **van.** It was a large closed **truck.**

vanilla

These are the pods of the **vanilla** plant.
The **vanilla** beans have a sweet smell and a lovely taste.

vase

This **vase** is a good shape for holding flowers.
It has a wide mouth to hold lots of stems.

vegetable

What is your favorite **vegetable?** My favorites are carrots and cauliflower.

vein

The rib of a leaf is its **vein.**
This leaf has large and small **veins.**

view

I like to look at the **view** from the window of a tall building. I can see almost the whole city.

Viking

This long, narrow ship is a **Viking ship.**
The **Vikings** sailed across the sea to the shores of America in ships like this.

village

This **village** lies in a peaceful valley.
A **village** is a small town.

vine

A **vine** is a plant with long stems that creep along the ground or climb up a wall. Ivy is a **vine.** Most melons grow on **vines.**

vinegar

Vinegar is a sour liquid that is used with oil in salad dressing.

violet

The **violet** is a small flower that grows wild or in gardens.
The scent of the **violet** is very nice.

violin

A string on Peter's **violin** is broken. A new string will have to be put in its place.

visit

Uncle George and Aunt May have come to pay us a **visit.**
They have brought my cousins Stephen and Diane with them.

vitamins

Vitamins are found in most foods we eat. They are very important in keeping us healthy.

voice

Our **voice** is the sound we make when we speak.

vote

Our class has decided to have a president to take charge of it. We will all **vote** for the pupil we want to be president.

voyage

Sandy and Sally are going to visit relatives in Europe.
It will be a long **voyage,** sailing across the sea.

 **W w**

wade

Mary Ann is too small to go into the swimming pool.
She is only allowed to **wade** in the shallow water.

wagon

George received a red **wagon** for Christmas. It has four wheels and a handle.

 **wallpaper**

This roll of **wallpaper** is the pattern we chose for our living room. It will be pasted up to cover the bare walls.

 **walrus**

The **walrus** is a large water animal.
It has flippers instead of feet, and two large tusks.

warm

I like the weather when it is **warm.**
It is not too hot and not too cold.

 **warn**

DANGER! KEEP AWAY. ICE UNSAFE!

Anthony is reading the sign that was put there to **warn** him. It tells him that the ice on the pond is thin.

246

wash

Lucy always makes a face when she has to **wash.** She hates washing in this small bowl.

wasp

A **wasp** is a stinging insect. **Wasps** live in papery-looking nests around the eaves of houses. Their bite is quite painful.

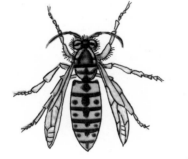

 ## watch

This is my first **watch.**
It is a **wristwatch.**
I already know how to tell time on it.

 ## water

We are lucky. When we need **water,** we simply turn the faucet.

 ## water

Mary is careful to **water** her flower garden every day.
Her father **waters** the lawn with a hose.

waterfall

When a river comes to a cliff, it plunges over the rocks in a **waterfall.**

water lily

The **water lily** is a plant with large white flowers that floats in ponds or lakes.

wave

We have been on a visit to Uncle George's farm. As the train leaves, we all **wave** good-by.

waves

The wind has whipped up the water of the ocean. This ship is steaming through high **waves.**

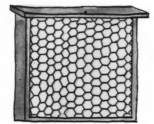

wax

This is a beehive. The beekeeper has taken the honey out of the honeycomb. What is left is **wax.**

weather

Elizabeth is listening for a **weather** report on the radio. She wants to know whether it will be sunny or rainy.

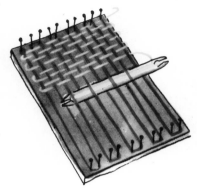

weave

This is my **weaving set.** I can **weave** cloth with it.

web

A **web** is a net of fine threads. Spiders built beautiful **webs** to catch insects.

Wednesday

Wednesday is the fourth day of the week. People who go to work call it the middle-of-the-week day.

weed

This is a thistle plant. It is called a **weed** because it is not wanted in gardens.

week

A **week** is seven days. This calendar shows that it is Saturday, the last day of the **week.**

welcome

When we are glad to see someone, we say they are **welcome.** If someone thanks us for something, we say "You are **welcome.**"

well

This is an old **well.**
The pail is at the bottom of the **well.**
When it is brought up, it will be full of water.

west

The **west** is the direction in which the sun sets.

wet

Evelyn does not like getting **wet.**
She is dressed for rainy weather.

whale

The **whale** is a sea animal.
It is one of the largest animals in the world.

wheat

Wheat is a very useful grain.
Ripe **wheat** is golden yellow.
From it we make flour.

whip

A **whip** is a strip of leather or cord.
When a wagon driver wants his horses
to go faster, he cracks his **whip.**

whisper

Dorothy knows a secret. She
will **whisper** it in her
brother's ear.
She will **speak softly** so no
one else can hear.

white

White is a color. It is the color of
newly fallen snow.

wide

The river is **wide** at this place. It will
take us a long time to reach the other
bank.

wild

An animal that lives in the forest or the jungle is a **wild** animal. It is **not tame.**

willow

This odd-looking tree is a **willow.** It is called a **basket willow** because its twigs are used to make baskets.

wind

The **wind** has blown Herbert's hat off. **Wind** is a rush of air.

window

These children are looking out a **window** of their new house. Some **windows** open outward. Others slide up and down.

wings

Birds and airplanes can fly because they have **wings.** The **wings** keep them up in the air.

winter

Winter is the season that begins in December. It is the coldest time of the year.

wire

This is a **wire fence.** The **wires** are twisted together so that nothing can get through.

wolf

The **wolf** is a wild animal. It is related to the dog.

wood

This table is made of **wood.** **Wood** comes from trees.

woodpecker

There is a hammering up in the tree. It is a **woodpecker** hunting for tiny insects to eat.

wool

Wool comes from sheep. It is woven into yarn and then wound into balls like this one. Mother is knitting with this **wool.**

word

A **word** is a sound that means something. This book is made up of **words** and pictures.

work

This man **works** in a factory. The machine helps him at his **work.**

world

The **world** is the earth. It is all the lands and all the seas.

worm

This **worm** lives in the earth. It makes tunnels for itself like hollow tubes.

wreath

At Christmas we put a holly **wreath** on the front door. It is a circle of little branches tied together.

wrinkle

A **wrinkle** is a small fold in cloth. Mother irons our clothes to remove the **wrinkles.**

wrist

The **wrist** is the joint between the hand and the arm. With the **wrist** we can move our hand in any direction.

write

This is how I **write.**
I **write** a letter to my friend.

X x · Y y · Z z

X-ray

An **X-ray** is a kind of picture. It shows our insides and helps the doctor find out what is wrong when we are sick.

yam

The **yam** is a plant like the sweet potato. It grows mainly in hot countries.

yarn

Yarn is a heavy thread. Mother uses cotton and wool **yarn** to knit and crochet.

year

A **year** is twelve months.
On this calendar it is December 31, the last day of the **year.**

yellow

Yellow is a color. It is the color of sunlight and the color of gold.

yolk

The **yolk** is the yellow part of an egg. When I have a boiled egg, I like for the **yolk** to be soft.

zebra

The **zebra** is a wild member of the horse family.
Zebras live in Africa.

zero

Zero is a number. It stands for **nothing.**

zinc

Zinc is a bluish white metal. It is used in making roofs. It is also used in medicines.

zipper

A **zipper** is a fastener with teeth that lock together.
We use **zippers** on all kinds of clothing and on boots.

zoo

The crocodile in our **zoo** has a waterhole of its own.
The **zoo** keeps all kinds of wild animals so that people can see what they look like close up.